DEDICATION

In memory of my cousin David Fallon.
26 Dec 1958 – 15 Nov 2019
Our world may feel your loss, especially your humour and laughter, but the Spirit world gained a lovable rogue who will undoubtedly cause mayhem and madness, but always with a smile.

CONTENTS

Acknowledgments	vii
Foreword	ix
Introduction	xi
Part I	1
1. Through Darkness to Light	3
2. Encouraging Words	9
3. No Escaping Grief	15
4. Losing David	23
Part II	31
5. Speaking Of Grief	33
6. Remembering	49
7. Lessons	58
8. Walking To The Light	78
Part III	125
9. Overcoming Grief	127
10. Processes Of Grief	136
PART IV	
Healing Through Mediumship	145
Helpful Organisations	155
About the Author	157

ACKNOWLEDGMENTS

I would like to express my grateful thanks to all those who kindly allowed me to tell their stories of how grief affected their lives, how they learned to cope and live with the loss of a loved one or dearly loved pet. There are many and some have chosen to remain anonymous; I fully understand their wishes. Some names have been changed to respect privacy.

My thanks go to Michele Taylor, Allessandra Pritchard, John O'Connell, Miriam and John Fitzgerald, Andrew Campbell Smith, Susan Dodd, Joanne Jones, Sandy Campbell, Irene Winton, Mhairi Kimmet, Anne Thomas, the Rev. Kathleen Hoffman and of course, those who chose to remain anonymous. My thanks to my cousin David's wife, Margaret Fallon, for kindly agreeing to what I have written in relation to my own emotions and thoughts on his passing and to my dedication at the start of the book.

I would also like to express my thanks to Minister Janet Parker for writing the foreword and for being an excellent tutor and friend.

FOREWORD

Those of you who read this book may be doing so because you feel in that state of darkness or you know it as a place you have been in.

Eleanor tries in her own logical and researched way to bring some light onto the subject of grief. Some will never get over loss, but Eleanor does show us that we can learn to live with it. The reader will be able to see that she has put a lot of thought into this book and her stories are not only interesting but, knowing Eleanor, I also see her stories as entertaining and you can see how this lady uses her own coping mechanism and her knowledge and love of the Spirit to help her move on with her life.

Spiritualist Minister
Janet Parker

INTRODUCTION

It took me a long time to write my first book *No Proof Required, Embracing my life as a Medium*. My thoughts were when I get round to writing the next book, it would be completed much quicker. I also seemed to be getting prompted to listen for the title which would come from my Spirit Guides. I soon heard the words "Through Darkness to Light". It sounded a bit harsh but my Spirit guides soon let me know that as we live in our physical world we are closer to darkness than the Light. It is in the learning of life's lessons that the Light within us grows and guides us towards the Eternal Light, the Light that is the Truth of our immortality. The essence of our very being, our Soul. It is forever connected to the Great Spirit, the source of all life, God.

The Spirit realms, our home, are where everyone returns to be welcomed back into the Light. The greatest time that we feel the darkness is when we lose someone we love. Death is a hard lesson for everyone, whether it is a person, a pet, a job, a limb or even the life we once knew. The darkness descends with the grief that threatens to suffocate us in sorrow and drown us in tears. Grief affects everyone differently and each person experi-

INTRODUCTION

ences varying stages. This darkness that grief brings will often shroud our memories and keep the pain of loss to the forefront of our minds and lives. Yet, as a medium, I know that Death is only the loss of the physical framework that encased our Soul, allowing it to journey through a life and learn, as if in a school. You see, death is birth. A Soul is birthed as a baby into this life, and so shall that Soul experience re-birth to the natural home in the realms of Spirit, where their light that was dimmed shall shine again.

It is this occurrence that Spirit encourages us to investigate and to see that there is a way to overcome the darkness and to reach for the Light. I have tried through my mediumship to bring the 'evidence' in messages from Spirit that life for every soul is eternal and that those loved ones lost are still very much alive and their Light and Love still exists. Though Mediumship may be of some help to those who grieve the loss of a loved one, it is not the complete answer as to how one can find a way through the darkness and eventually become capable of living as normally as they can. The loss of a job, a limb or even a lifestyle can and does affect our lives and how we cope, often not realising that we are, in fact, grieving.

The stages of grief affect everyone, although many experience these stages over varying periods of time. Even animals grieve the loss of their human or animal companion. It is said there are many stages such as Denial, Anger, Bargaining, Depression and Acceptance. I am sure there are many more. When these stages begin to become ever present with no sign of abating, the situation can quickly develop into Post Traumatic Stress Disorder which can be life threatening. It is then that help is required and careful monitoring of the grieving person is paramount.

One death can trigger memories of deaths in the past that may have seen grief suppressed. This heightens the darkness that begins to overwhelm the person who is missing the phys-

INTRODUCTION

ical presence of their loved one. In some circumstances, grief, when identified, may be hard to accept. Learning to adapt in a way that allows life to resume can be daunting.

To someone who is unable to see a way forward from grief, the thought of suicide becomes a solution, and sadly this does happen.

Mediumship is first and foremost a healing modality. It is a gift that should be used responsibly and with compassion. It is a wonderful feeling when I bring forward a message from a loved one in Spirit, which is so profound and full of Love that the change in the recipient is blatantly obvious. To see a person grow in stature from someone who was huddled in sorrow and pain to a bright and smiling person ready to live again knowing their loved one is safe and well, watching over them, is more than enough reward.

It also helps someone, who felt their last action or words to a dying relative or friend were harsh and unkind, when they are given a chance to apologise and express their remorse. This works too for the Spirit communicator.

The darkness of this life is prevalent in many ways. As we are born into this life we learn by facing challenges and overcoming difficulties. We were never issued with a set of instructions or guidelines. It is puzzling at times when I see the destruction and devastation that occurs in our world, the terrible tragedies and dreadful crimes against people, animals and even lands. Yet each of us are born with an internal light, the Light of our Soul. My own understanding is that we are meant to let our Light shine. Love is the battery that keeps our Light shining and draws to us those in Spirit who continue to love us, no matter what.

It is not just the death of a loved one that may cause us to grieve, there are many losses that trigger grief. Some may feel the loss of a pet which was a constant companion. It could even be the loss of mobility through illness or accident. It could even be the loss of contact with family or a friend through disagreements. The loss of a job through retirement can often leave a gaping hole in someone's life, which sees them feeling abandoned or even feeling no longer of use. Worse still the loss of access to a child through a relationship break up or divorce can cause immense grief to a parent or guardian. Examples of the type of grief that this brings can be seen in a television programme called "Long Lost Family". The grief and destruction of a life is clearly seen in the episodes that tell of family separations and even abandonment. Some people spend years trying to come to terms with such a loss. They never fully experience full happiness or contentment. It is not only their emotional and mental health that suffers, but their physical abilities often show the strain and manifest in illness and sometimes death from a broken heart. This programme is a platform which displays vividly the hurt and pain felt by those affected, whether the loss or separation was through circumstances which they had no choice in or because they were unable to provide or care for a child. It is heart-warming to see the joy on the faces of those who are re-united. Sadly, sometimes the reconciliation is through the knowledge that love and memories survived even though death may have prevented a physical reunion. No-one truly knows what someone goes through unless they too have experienced such a loss. We often rush through life's challenges and forget to feel grateful for the time with, and the presence of, our loved ones. It is when their physical departure occurs that we begin to realise the part they played in our lives.

At times of loss darkness seeps in and changes our outlook and our ability to see the Light. Mediumship is not the cure but it may provide the trigger that brings answers and helps us through these situations. This may seem strange to someone who opposes mediumship or lacks any knowledge of its existence but I know from experience that it can and does help. You

INTRODUCTION

do not need to experience death or any other loss to find some benefit from communication with a loved one in Spirit. Our loved ones who dwell in the world of Spirit still care for us and will stay close and will do everything they can to bring comfort, support and guidance, especially in times of sadness, trauma, mental and emotional difficulties.

It is my hope that the stories, words and information contained within this book will be of some comfort to the reader.

PART I

THROUGH DARKNESS TO LIGHT

My first book *No Proof Required, Embracing my life as a Medium*, was as challenging as exciting to write. It brought back many memories some good, some happy and some sad. Once finished and self-published I felt relieved. It had taken me a long time to finally complete it. Yet I had a sense of pride when I held the first copy in my hand. I was grateful too, for the guidance and encouragement from family and friends, and of course my Spirit teachers and guides.

For many it is difficult to understand that we are Spirit born into this physical world to learn life's lessons and that the Light we all hold within us grows and guides us towards the Eternal Light; the Light that is the Truth of our immortality, which is the essence of our very being, our Soul. It is forever connected to the Great Spirit, the source of all life, God if you will. Through this life we will experience darkness, especially at times of loss. It is in those times when we need to find a way through to the light, in order to find comfort and peace. This is where my abilities as a Medium can be of profound assistance to those who grieve.

The Spirit realms, our home, are where everyone returns to be welcomed back into the Light. The greatest time that we feel the darkness is when we lose someone we love. Death is a hard lesson for everyone, whether it is a person, a pet, a job or even a limb. The darkness descends with the grief that threatens to suffocate us in sorrow and drown us in tears. Grief affects everyone differently and each person experiences varying stages. This darkness that grief brings will often shroud our memories and keep the pain of loss to the forefront of our minds and lives. Yet, as a medium, I know that Death is only the loss of the physical framework that encased our Soul, allowing it to journey through a life and learn, as if in a school. You see - death is birth. A Soul is birthed as a baby into this life, and so shall that Soul experience re-birth to the natural home in the realms of Spirit, where their light that was dimmed shall shine again.

It is this occurrence that Spirit encourages us to investigate and to see that there is a way to overcome the darkness and to reach for the Light. I have tried, through my mediumship, to bring the information, or evidence if you like, that life for every Soul is eternal and that those loved ones lost are still very much alive and that their Light and Love still exists. Though Mediumship may be of some help to those who grieve the loss of a loved one, it is not the answer as to how one can find a way through the darkness and eventually become capable of living as normally as they can. The loss of a job, a limb or even a lifestyle can and does affect our lives and how we cope, often not realising that we are, in fact, grieving.

The stages of grief affect everyone, although many experience these stages over varying periods of time. Even animals grieve the loss of their human or animal companion. It is said there are many stages such as Denial, Anger, Bargaining, Depression and Acceptance. I am sure there are many more. When these stages begin to become ever present with no sign of abating, the situation can quickly develop into Post Traumatic Stress Disorder which can be life threatening. It is then that help is required and careful monitoring of the grieving person is paramount. One death can trigger memories of deaths in the past that may have seen grief suppressed, and this heightens the darkness that begins to overwhelm the person who is missing the physical presence of their loved one. Grief, when identified, may be hard to accept in some circumstances. Learning to adapt in a way that allows life to resume can be daunting. To someone who is unable to see a way forward from grief, the thought of suicide becomes a solution, and sadly this does happen.

Mediumship is first and foremost a healing modality. It is a gift that should be used responsibly and with compassion. It is a wonderful feeling when I bring forward a message from a loved one in Spirit, which is so profound and full of Love that the change in the recipient is blatantly obvious. To see a person grow in stature from someone who was huddled in sorrow and pain to a bright and smiling person ready to live again knowing their loved one is safe and well, watching over them, is more than enough reward.

It also helps, someone who felt their last action or words to a dying relative or friend, were harsh and unkind, when they are given a chance to apologise and express their remorse. This works too for the Spirit communicator.

The darkness of this life is prevalent in many ways. As we are born into this life we learn by facing challenges and overcoming difficulties. We were never issued a set of instructions or guidelines. It is puzzling at times when I see the destruction and devastation that occurs in our world, the terrible tragedies and dreadful crimes against people and lands. Yet each of us was born with an internal light, the Light of our Soul. My own understanding is that we are meant to let our light shine. Love is the battery that keeps our Light shining and draws to us those in Spirit who continue to Love us no matter what.

It is not just the death of a loved one that may cause us to grieve. There are many losses that trigger grief: some may feel the deep loss of a pet who was a constant companion; the loss of mobility through illness or accident; the loss of family or friend through a silly disagreement or argument. The loss of a job through retirement can often leave a gaping hole in someone's life, which sees them feeling abandoned or even feeling no longer of use. At these times, darkness seeps in and changes our outlook and our ability to see the Light. Mediumship is not the cure but it may provide the trigger that brings answers and helps us through these situations.

How do we overcome or at least cope with grief and try to move on with our lives?

I recall my own mother's death which was very sudden and unexpected. She was a very active woman and worked long hours as our family Doctor's receptionist. The telephone call to my place of work really shocked me. I was sure my colleague had made a mistake when she said my mother had been taken to hospital suffering from a heart attack. She was in her fifties - not old by any means. My father had suffered angina and other illnesses and my initial reaction was it must be him who had been taken to hospital. A visit to the hospital proved me wrong.

My mother seemed to recover and was allowed home, but less than a week later she was dead. The memory remains clear in my mind as if it was yesterday rather than thirty-eight years ago. When she was released from hospital my mother commented to me that she would love to visit the Trossachs, a beautiful area of Scotland. A strange request but one I was able to fulfil for her. During that trip my mother and I had a strange conversation. In it I told her that death is nothing to fear and that the Spirit world is a far better place than where we are on earth. She seemed to be afraid of death. She listened to me but I was not sure I had said the right thing. Grief affects us in so many ways and no two people will ever suffer the same effects. I know that, for two years after my mother's death, my life had no real meaning and I was just going through the motions of eating, sleeping and working. Tears fell easily and often. It was many years later, after developing my mediumship, that I realised how our conversation had actually been a great help to her.

I have come across many people who have lost loved ones: some through long drawn out illnesses; others through accidents; and sadly, some through the act of suicide. There are, of course, the strange cases of deaths that are never really explained or understood. Cot deaths and sudden deaths are hard to accept. How sad it is when a cot death occurs. Parents, who are only just settling into a new way of life with the gift of a child, suddenly find themselves bereft at the sudden loss of their baby. I recall an incident very early on in my career as a police officer where I attended a very distressing scene. A house full of happy people celebrating; baby asleep in upstairs bedroom. In an instant, all changes when a check on the baby reveals he has been sick and is not breathing. My colleagues and I were just passing in our patrol car. My intuitive side was strong and made me aware of the chaos and that something was wrong. I insisted my colleague turn our vehicle around and go to the house. We had no sooner turned when someone ran out the house, waving and calling for help. I can still see the scene. An ambulance was called and my colleagues and I ran up to the bedroom. The baby was still alive and one of my colleagues began CPR. To this day I can still see the sick on the wall and see that baby boy's face change from pink to grey. Even the ambulance men could not save the baby. I had the terrible task of telling the mother that her baby boy was dead. That wee baby boy's name and that house have remained in my memory and often comes back into my mind. The grief must have been overwhelming and I wonder how the young couple coped. My Spirit guide tells me that the baby would have been cared for as he grew in Spirit. Yet I question the purpose of such a death.

ENCOURAGING WORDS

I find at times my Spirit friends bring forward their words, sometimes in the form of poems to help those who grieve. Among the Spirit guides who help me are Chang-Li and Ramain, both who possess such wisdom and exude kindness and compassion. They never fail to answer any questions or doubts I may have.

Quite often they impress in my mind the solutions to my thoughts on grief and how I can be of help to someone who is suffering loss.

From Spirit:

"Many have felt such grief, and many have come to see that it is a symptom of the condition you call Death. Be assured that nothing will prevent the passage of the Soul into our realms. Do not despair for the one who is lost to you, for they are welcomed home with much rejoicing. It is sad for you in your physical world especially as you do not see as we do, that you do not feel as we do and that you do not have the Faith that we do. Just as you chose to be born into the physical, you too shall be born again into the Spirit, your true home, the home of your Creator. We ask that you remember that, as you chose the physical experience, you must be aware that not all challenges will bring happi-

ness but that you will also be prone to the sadness, madness and badness that exists in the physical. All are lessons that your Soul will be asked to learn. How you learn and how you overcome the different challenges will be a testament to your Soul's courage and adaptability. All we wish for every Soul is that they learn Love, to give, to receive, to share. For it is Love that will take them Through Darkness to Light."

Blessings Chang-Li

Can we begin to imagine the grief that others feel? I doubt it. The way people grieve is personal to each and every one. As a medium I find it very hard at times to understand the tragedies that befall some families. Though I have suffered grief at the loss of my loved ones, my knowledge and belief in the Spirit realms has helped me immensely, but it has never stopped the hurt or the tears from falling. I still find myself asking my Spirit guides for help in understanding a particular catastrophe where many lives have been lost.

From Spirit:
"My Dear One, it is with compassion we speak as we try to comfort those who are suffering the pain and sorrow of such tragedies. We watch you as you struggle to understand the scale of such losses. You may not be party to what occurs at the moment of these deaths but we assure you that all is well with each individual Soul as it leaves the physical body. We hear your cry as you question the purpose. Whether the passing is gentle or violent, it does not matter a jot, for each Soul is welcomed with its needs attended to. A time of rest may be required, while a time of continuous sleep may be needed for some. Until the Souls can comprehend and accept their new life, they are nurtured with Love. When that moment arrives, they release their earthly

anguish. Many are present, known and unknown, ready to rejoice with each and every Soul. All are welcomed into the home of their Creator."

Ramain

I see your tears
I try so hard
To calm your fears
I may not be
So present now
But I can see
Through the veil somehow
You call my name
And wonder why
I had to leave
I had to die
Yet here I am
Free of pain
Alive and well
Full of joy again
So now I say
My Love is strong
And sent to you
To guide you along
That you may know
Love never parts
And death cannot divide
Our two loving hearts
Be not afraid
In your time of sorrow
There will always be

> A new tomorrow
> Our many memories
> Will ease your pain
> Till time passes on
> And we meet again.

I shared this verse on the social media site, Facebook. I was overwhelmed at the response from so many people who were grieving at the time. Some sent me lovely comments to say how these words had helped or inspired them as they grieved.

It is my hope in writing this book that the words from my Spirit friends and guides will bring comfort, healing and the knowledge that death is not the end but a doorway to eternal life.

Trying to carry on living after a death can be extremely tiring and many of us seem to feel that time stands still. Days and nights drag. The time immediately after a death is usually filled with notifying many people and organisations, then registering the death and making funeral arrangements. Visitors come and go, and depending on how the death occurred, there can even be legal processes to go through which often adds to the distress and anxiety. It is heart-breaking and sometimes downright confusing. The death of a child brings terrible sadness and feelings of inadequacy, with thoughts of having failed in the care of the child. Many questions that may be difficult to answer swim round in the heads of the parents and other family members. The grief that is felt is overwhelming. Life for some stops as their grief is all consuming. The various stages of grief can suck every ounce of energy from the body, leaving those grieving with a sense that life is not fair or worse still, not worth living. Depression may take over and mental health issues surface as the darkness slowly engulfs the light of life.

As depressing as my words may be, they are true and this is where I hope my Spirit guides can help. Having the gift of mediumship does not dissolve the sensitivity to grief nor does it make it easier to cope. It does, however, give comfort in the knowledge that Death is a doorway to eternal life where every Soul is welcomed home.

No-one can ever know what it feels like to walk in someone else's shoes when they are experiencing death of a loved one or animal. It is so individual and unique to each person. The mind configures differently in everyone. Some people may find it easier to cry alone while others let their tears flow freely.

Often methods are used to hide feelings - working hard, concentrating on keeping busy - yet the memories do not go away. The stage we call Acceptance is critical to kick-start a path to healing.

> The wind of change becomes a gale
> We know not where our feelings stray
> Or even if night is day
> Time stands still like a broken clock
> Caught in a cradle that will not rock
> The darkness follows like a shadow
> Clinging to hope frightened to let go
> Days pass like a horror story
> The trauma continues waving a flag of glory
> No depth to reach for the pain
> As waves of hurt flow again and again
> The endless nights drag life down
> While constant tears threaten to drown
> All memories to make us smile
> Screaming out loud is life worthwhile
> So, on that lonely road you walk
> Just open a door start to talk

Someone may know how black is despair
A broken heart needs someone to care
Let out the anger, frustration and fear
Give voice to the rage inside that you hear
Speak of the guilt and every feeling
For this is a way to the journey of healing
Allowing you to rise from the ashes of death
Facing tomorrow with exuberant breath
When Grief takes over there's a battle to win
Though acceptance is hard, life again will begin.

NO ESCAPING GRIEF

What is it that defines Grief? That's a question that as yet I know of no reasonable answer. A person may begin to grieve the moment they are told their loved one has a terminal illness and there is no hope of survival. Others may find that after the death they feel relief rather than grief. This is true if the illness has been long drawn out and their loved one suffered much pain. They may even have felt completely exhausted after looking after their loved one on a daily and nightly basis. The initial passing away may come as a massive lifting of responsibility from the shoulders of the carer. A feeling of freedom may permeate the mind of the carer, knowing that their duty has been completed and now they themselves can rest and be able to continue life without worrying if their loved one is ok. On the other hand, someone who has spent many months, maybe even years, caring for a loved one may find themselves at a loss as to how to integrate back into a normal life. They may find themselves slipping into a depressed state through grief not just brought on by the death of the loved one, but through changes to everyday life caused by loss.

Many people who have lost a loved one often find themselves thinking - where are they? Are they safe? Is there a heaven or place they have gone to? Will I see them again when I come to die? My own belief system based around Spiritualism and the knowledge that life after physical death goes on is a great source of help to me. I do understand that others who have conventional religious ideas may consider this to be hocus pocus and a way to appease the grieving heart and mind.

Within this book I hope to bring messages from Spirit to comfort and also to share the stories of some who have come to terms with the journey of grief or are still walking in the darkness. Hopefully I can encourage Light back into the lives of those who are struggling with their mental, physical and emotional health through the process of grief.

First let me start with my own story. The first death that seemed to affect me was the death of a lovely friend. He was the brother of my boyfriend at the time. A nicer lad you could not have met. He was engaged to be married. Tragically, he died in a car accident that happened just outside my place of work. I remember my mother telling me about it as she knew his parents. I was not at work that day or I would have witnessed the accident as it occurred at a time when I would have been leaving to go home. There was a photo taken at the accident scene on the front page of the local newspaper. I kept this in my purse for a long time. Initially he was said to be alright and had sat up in his hospital bed speaking with his family. Sadly, later that night, a blood clot travelled to his heart causing his death.

My mother called at the family home to pass on our condolences. She didn't think it a good idea for me to view his body and suggested I remember him as he was when I last saw him. My sister often tells of how I cried for many hours after his death. I was unaware of the effect grief was having on me and I found myself crying easily. I had an item of his in my bag which I had to return to his family as they wanted to put it in his coffin. This felt like another blow to me as I would hold this item when I cried. My relationship with his brother did not last long but my memories of this death remained with me for a very long time. The photo of the accident has long been lost, but to this day I can still see the crumpled wreckage and the snow falling heavy over the vehicle. It was the weather conditions that seemed to have caused the accident rather than any fault of the drivers.

Not many years passed before I knew grief again at the sudden loss of my mother. She died at only fifty seven years of age. Far too young. It was especially difficult as she had been in reasonably good health before suffering a heart attack. She had often suffered bouts of pleurisy which caused her to need time away from her work. She came home from hospital and was feeling good and thinking of going back to work. My Mother had once told me she would love to visit the Trossachs, a beautiful part of Scotland. This was arranged and we stopped off at a bar to have some lunch. I have never forgotten what my mother said to me. Her words were,

"Why didn't you tell me that I nearly died?"

My mother obviously knew I was aware of Spirit but never encouraged me for fear of ridicule; plus, she didn't believe in the Spirit world. I answered her saying,

"I couldn't tell you that when you were lying all wired up to all sorts of machines." I went on to say to her,

"Mum, you have nothing to fear, you will be going to a better place."

. . .

My mother died of another massive heart attack a few days later. For many years I regretted saying these words to her, thinking if I had not spoken them she would have fought harder to live. My mother's death greatly affected the Doctor who raced to our house when he was advised that my mother had been found collapsed. My mother had helped him from the day he joined the practice as a young locum. He returned to the surgery, went into his room and could be heard crying by the other receptionist. Grief consumed me. I was lost, suffering bouts of insecurity, depression and anger. I was married at the time and my husband told me he had no idea how to cope with me. He would tell me my mother would come to me in a dream and let me know she was alright. I would wake each morning upset that I hadn't seen my mother in a dream. I took time off work as I tried to overcome my grief. It took many years. Not even the birth of my daughter, a year after Mum died, could take my sadness away.

My father struggled terribly after her death. Mum was always there to keep him on the straight and narrow, especially when alcohol was involved. He had been a prisoner of war in Changi, Singapore and had been tortured and starved. His memories and flashbacks caused him nightmares, not to mention stomach problems. He had to have half his stomach removed as a result of his treatment in Changi prison. With Mum gone he turned to alcohol and died ten years later. My sister and I had tried to help him but he just drank himself to death. Being older and more in tune with Spirit, his death didn't affect me in the same way as Mum's. Although I was sad I knew he would once again be with Mum and the son they lost at three months old, born before my sister and me.

Although working with Spirit is helpful it does not give us any more protection from death or the grief that envelopes us.

THROUGH DARKNESS TO LIGHT

. . .

The difference between the deaths of Mum and Dad was very strange for me. With Mum's passing I really struggled. I would often be unable to concentrate on what I should be doing or I would forget what it was I had been looking for. I was irritable and wasn't open to sympathy or hugs from anyone. At times, I was angry and felt Mum's death was unfair as she was not old.

Her own mother, the only Grandparent I knew, was still living although she was suffering from dementia. I remember when she was brought to the house to see Mum on the day of the funeral. Gran didn't seem to be aware that Mum was lying in her coffin. Gran began looking in bedside drawers and was annoyed when she found something that she felt was hers and said, "Why has our Peggy got my stuff?" I can laugh at this now but at the time it was difficult to understand. My Mum died on Easter Monday which was 20th April that year. Gran died on Easter Monday the following year. I was more aware of my Spiritual abilities by then and spooked my sister when she called the Friday before to say Gran was not expected to live through the night. I told my sister that Gran would die on the Monday which was Easter Monday. When it came to pass, my sister was so annoyed at me, demanding to know how I knew. She never has quite believed in my abilities.

With Gran and Dad's death I was more settled, knowing that all would be well and they would be living on within the realms of Spirit. It did not stop me from missing Dad - I never felt particularly close to Gran.

. . .

So you see, Grief has a way of affecting everyone. It can bring a sense of desolation and fear to those left behind.

The cause of a death can greatly increase the symptoms of grief. When a death has been the result of an accident, suicide or as the result of a crime, it is sudden and unexpected. This in itself, brings added sorrow and hurt, making the death very hard to accept and grief becomes overwhelming. Many feel rage, resentment, guilt, blame and even have thoughts of revenge. Some have become suicidal and find themselves in dire need of help, often not knowing who to turn to. Senseless loss of a life is often unbearable for the family, friends and workmates, who try hard to understand the 'whys' and 'if onlys'.

I know that it is not only the loss of a loved one that can fill us with despair and grief. The loss of a beloved pet or animal can be just as soul destroying, leaving the owner distraught. The phrase "it's only a dog/cat/animal" is of no help to someone grieving such a loss. It only amplifies that the speaker has no real sense of compassion or has never felt the love and bond between animal and human. The physical presence of our loved one is gone and it leaves not only an empty space in our lives but in our hearts.

Think how much harder grief can affect those who have lost a loved one, not through death, but as a result of the person or animal having gone missing. Lives seem to come to a standstill and grief, with its different symptoms, becomes all consuming. Many left to grieve simply give up and die of a broken heart. The hardest thing is the not knowing what happened to them, whether they are suffering, lying injured, being treated badly or dead. These thoughts can play so many tricks on the mind. The hurt and pain seems to be multiplied as each day, month and year passes without a glimmer of hope. How do you mourn the loss when someone or some beloved animal is missing? Does one know they are grieving?

To mourn the death of a loved one is to recognise that they are no longer physically with us. Their part in our life has ceased to be. Mourning takes many forms. Some religions will see that the body is buried or cremated instantly, while others may take days or weeks to complete the funeral process. Some wear black while others wish the life to be celebrated with the wearing of bright colours. Dealing with death is a very personal experience. Personally, as a spiritualist, being aware that the essence of a person, or soul if you wish, lives on in the Spirit realms is a comfort. The body has been cast off and conditions that were present are released, allowing the etheric form to live on. The conscious mind is eternal. This may bring comfort but it will never stop the pain of losing a loved one or pet.

As individual as we all are, we will undergo a number of symptoms that come with grief and loss. Feelings of sadness, despair, anger, pain, guilt, blame and hopelessness are just a few that rear their heads when we find grief has taken over our lives. The saying "Time heals" doesn't cut the mustard when grief suffocates our senses leaving a void that just won't be filled with words of comfort or encouragement.

The early days after a death or loss are filled with questions, doubts and uncertainty. Then comes the need to arrange a funeral or disposal of a pet's body. If the loss is of another nature, confusion may reign as to how one will deal with the future. Some may feel there is no future and find that their thoughts are filled with ways to end their own life. Many tend to become isolated and think they are shielding themselves from more hurt. They may even try to shield others from their sorrow, not wanting to feel reliant or pitied.

The loss of a limb, job, friendship or an expected lifestyle are other causes of grief and again bring many symptoms which others will fail to understand. Someone who suffers grief in these situations will have the added symptoms of failure, inadequacy or feelings of unworthiness.

There are many stages of grief to consider and the ability to cope and to recover to an extent where life has some normality, stretches each individual's strength and resilience. The love and help of family and friends is vital at such times.

Each individual case can bring to light different actions, non-actions and reactions to the loss suffered. The physical, mental, emotional and spiritual strength of the person left to grief will play an important part in their ability to handle, cope and to recover. The very real task of picking up and facing life again will rely on some, or all, of these strengths.

LOSING DAVID

As mentioned earlier, in my own recovery, my sense and understanding of our immortality was of comfort to me as I knew my mother, father, my friends and pets were all very much alive in the Spirit world.

One death that caused me to shed many tears was the passing of my cousin David - he, his brothers Peter and John, and I were brought up together. David developed a sore leg which was eventually found to be cancerous. His leg was amputated but the cancer returned, spreading to his lungs. I relate David's story here.

The passing of my cousin David affected me profoundly. Younger than me by almost five years, he was always smiling, telling silly jokes, often unable to speak the punchline because he was laughing so much. Life was a breeze. Then came the news that he had cancer in his shin bone. It was necessary to amputate his leg above the knee. My own intuitive thoughts had felt that amputation would definitely be required but David said his consultant had told him that this would be the last option.

My gut instinct was torturing me, I knew he would not survive cancer. How I prayed that I was wrong. On the day of his operation I travelled through to the hospital. It was difficult seeing the pain etched on his face, yet after his leg was removed the relief from the pain was clearly visible. David had some respite and was doing well. I was looking forward to my daughter's wedding in October, when we would all be together. David, his wife Margaret, his younger brother John and his wife were all travelling to attend.

I kept in touch on social media and visited him in hospital and the hospice. On the day of the wedding David wore a fabulous kilted outfit and though he looked good, I could see he was not himself. I knew instantly, he was not going to survive this cancer.

The last time I saw David he was in hospital. It was a shock to see him so poorly. He gave us all a fright that night as he seemed to take a seizure. His wife held his right hand while I held his left. He settled eventually and as I left his hospital room, I told him I would bring him a stick of rock from Cyprus. I was due to travel there a few day later to see a football game between Scotland and Cyprus. I never saw David alive again. He passed to Spirit two days before I was due to fly home from Cyprus. His brother John had notified me that he was very poorly. I wanted to fly home but John said to stay and go to the football game. The next message from John told me David had died. I was so hurt. I went into my bedroom and cried. On two occasions when I was in Cyprus, I found myself writing what I felt regarding David. My words are below,

. . .

November 2019 in Larnaca, Cyprus

"The knowledge that a much loved cousin is dying has brought my thoughts into perspective regarding the work I do in performing services at Spiritualist churches and centres. As a working medium I am well aware of my responsibilities as I speak the words of a discarnate. To watch my cousin struggle to breathe as he battles lung cancer is to feel utterly inadequate and of no use to him. Feelings of despair remind me that I have no right to feel sad or hurt, or to even cry. It is not me who has the oxygen mask over my mouth and nose. It is not me who lies in the hospital bed fighting for breath, yet the sorrow that strikes me deep in my heart is disabling. It is piercing my whole being, depriving me of sensitivity as I feel the tears sting my eyes. What right do I have to wallow in self-pity as he lies close to death? It is my love for him that steadily penetrates my thoughts, punching through the veil of misery that threatens to overwhelm me. Recalling the last time I saw him in hospital I am reminded of the urge I had to run out of the hospital and cry out WHY? IT'S SO UNFAIR! I remember thinking how he needs normality, to know his devoted family are there, caring as always, desperately trying to give him peace in the knowledge he is not alone. The medium in me is keen to help, to talk to him, to let him know there is no blackness to overcome, but Light. A light that is pure Love illuminating his path to the arms of those he loved in another time, who await his arrival to lead him home, to eternal life, where pain is overcome and breathing is no longer a struggle.

Knowing I am unable to impart this knowledge becomes a burden within the grief that I experience while waiting for the news of his death.

Is grief an enemy or bedfellow, maybe both, for this state of suspended wisdom? My path is as unclear as his. Yet here I am, desperate to take his pain away and to release his fear so that he may step forward into his new journey, leaving behind a now useless body to be buried or cremated in a final farewell for family, who shall feel the sting of tears and the deep void his absence leaves.

Yet it is in the strength of Love that we experience the darkness of death, which overshadows life - life that continues, although I and many would want it to stop, even reverse and take the pain and reality of these moments back to a normal state where all was well. Sadly, within the heart, grief displays so clearly that such action is never possible. Through life we learn lessons, we grow, and we gain wisdom even though the lesson may be hard and difficult to accept. I feel the lesson for me with David's impending death is to love him in the moment until there are no more moments and all is still.

I think about the next time I will stand on a platform and speak the words of a discarnate. Will I feel the same? Shall I love enough to do justice to those who have made their final journey, yet wish their voice to be heard and their gift of Love to be returned to those they left behind? It is a responsibility that should never be shirked for, as I know, there is life and there is death, and while grief may deny us the knowledge of eternal life, it cannot smother the truth."

The news eventually came that David had died. It was hard to hear as I was still in Cyprus and felt sad that I would never see him again in this life. Once again I wrote the words of how I felt.

Larnaca, Cyprus 16 November 2019

"As I write the tears sting my eye, blurring my vision, making my face wet and my senses heightened. My mind is playing tricks telling me I have no right to cry, making me feel guilty for not being there when he died.

It's just less than an hour since I received the text message from John: DAVID PASSED AWAY. NOW PAIN FREE.

My emotions are overtaking my every thought. I stop crying. I think of how he will be free of this horrible illness, no longer struggling to breathe, no longer trying to be cheerful through the constant pain. Then I cry again and hear inside my head the screams of IT'S SO UNFAIR. Trying to compose myself I answer the text to let John know how heartbroken I am. I know his wife Margaret, his sons, his family and everyone who knew him will be too.

My knowledge of Spirit and my work as a Spirit medium is not of any help at this time as tears flow freely and my heart breaks even more. The guilt increases as I recall my prayers the evening before asking God to ease his passing, to take him home and out of the pain, to help his family as they watch him pass away before their eyes. To ease their pain too.

Now I feel in my heart that maybe I was wrong. Should I have prayed for his healing instead? Grief overwhelms the senses and crushes reason, almost forbidding rationality. It smothers any sense of relief that David has been set free of his pain and has made the journey home, into the arms of those he loved, gone before and waiting with outstretched arms to welcome him back into their Love, their world of eternal life"

As I calm down I recall my last words to David and realise that only the day before I had purchased that stick of Cyprus rock I had promised him.

As soon as I could I went to see his family. I was full of mixed emotions, sadness at his death and excited as David had come to me and said,

"Tell our John that I am alright."

That was all he said, but the smile on his face told me he was well. I had tried to speak with him but he was gone as soon as he spoke the words. I passed this message to John as we sat alone at his dining table. I had not wanted to say anything to his wife Margaret as I felt she was not ready. I knew, and I am certain David also knew that Margaret may not believe me. I feel certain David will get a message to her and it would be better if it comes from someone who has no knowledge of them.

The day of the funeral went by in a blur. The crematorium was filled to capacity. I don't think they had ever seen so many people at a funeral. Many friends had attended wearing David Bowie T-shirts. David was a massive fan of Mr Bowie and his music, often attending Bowie conventions. He even received a message from the Bowie family wishing him well as he fought the cancer. How strange that he died of the same disease as his idol. I do hope he meets him in Spirit. I am sure Mr Bowie will be laughing at David's' silly jokes. David made us all laugh one more time at the funeral as the last song to be played as we all left the crematorium was *Who wants to live forever?* Make them all laugh in Spirit, David.

Weeks, then months, went by and I seemed to struggle with his passing. One moment I was ok, then the next I was in tears, feeling I was caught in a nightmare and that I would wake up and it will all have just been a bad dream. Then I would recall my last visit to David in hospital and the tears would flow again. On one occasion, David woke me from sleep calling my name. He had a particular way of speaking my name. He never pronounced it as Eleanor, it was always Elnur. In my mind I could see him smiling. He was young and had his unruly hair. Although I felt sad it made me smile, reminding me of how he was, bringing back memories of how we played as children and how we grew into adults. I recalled a time when my Father was driving us to Ayr. As we approached the town we passed a cemetery. My Dad pointed to it and said,

"That's the dead centre of Ayr!"

Quick as a flash David piped up.

"A lot of people are dying to get in there!"

We all laughed. I still find it hard to believe he is gone from our world but I know he is well and cared for in Spirit. As I struggled with his death I would ask my Spirit guides questions about death and they would always respond by saying death is the doorway to eternal life and to our true home. They suggested I should see anniversaries of passings as birthdays in Spirit. So David, when the first anniversary of your death comes round I will wish you Happy Birthday.

Though my own grief is still affecting me I know that some people take different pathways to find a sense of normality that allows them to go on living.

Many will immerse themselves in work, while others will focus on something that takes their mind away from the memories, especially of the time their loved one or pet died. Individually we all react in our own way, dealing with grief as we try to understand exactly what and how we are feeling. Some are unable to cope and become depressed or even suicidal. As much as I would like to, I do not have the answers. Even as a medium it is hard to contemplate the agony and sadness someone is experiencing. I try to work with Spirit in a way that brings comfort, healing, love and even laughter to a recipient of a message from Spirit. I know through my work that our loved ones wish only one thing, and that is to let their family, friends and workmates know that they have survived the condition we call death and that they are well and cared for in the etheric realms. After that, they usually give encouragement and ask of their loved ones to live life without regrets, and to always remember that Love never dies and that one day they will meet again

PART II

SPEAKING OF GRIEF

The stories included in this part of the book are a testament to how people have found a way out of their darkness and into the Light of life after suffering a loss.

Some of the following cases reveal how the symptoms of grief can and will change the life of the person left to deal with their emotions.

This case involved the tragic death of a young man and the love of a mother who knows but can't explain why she has a weird feeling on the day she is told her son is in a coma. Her instinct has her reaching out to her son, trying to contact him by phone without success. Then her phone rings but it is not her son. The lady is called Irene, her son Paul. Irene explains how her son Paul was an active, energetic and loving son. He was very much into keeping fit and worked in security. Then the day came when what she describes as 'a weird feeling' come over her and wouldn't leave. She desperately tried to call her son without success.

These are her words.

IRENE'S STORY

"I recall the day the phone rang and I was told my son Paul was in a coma. I'd had a weird feeling all day. I can't describe it. I had received a text message from Paul in the morning to wish me Happy Birthday.

I went to lunch with a friend but still had the weird feeling. I tried to phone Paul in the afternoon but there was no reply. Once home I began to tidy up around the house. It was after dinner that the phone rang. It was Paul's friend. He said,

"Irene, Paul is in Edinburgh Royal Infirmary, he's in a coma."
"What happened, was he in a fight? I asked.
"No", he said, "it was attempted suicide."
I was struck dumb. Then I replied,
"No, he wouldn't do that, he sent me a text this morning."

When I got through to Edinburgh there were tubes coming out of Paul, he was bloated and didn't look like my boy. The consultant took me to a small room and gave me the news that Paul's brain had been starved and it would be better to let nature take its course. I was in shock and said that I wouldn't get my son back. To this the consultant answered - no.

I was in shock, disbelief, denial and angry. WHY had no-one called me to let me know what Paul had been doing?

In my state of shock and grief I lashed out at Paul's father. Why didn't he keep in touch with Paul? I suppose I was looking for someone to blame.

For six weeks my heart was breaking. The last time I went through to Edinburgh, it was to talk with the consultant. When I went into Paul's room, he gave me the biggest smile and my heart leapt. I rushed to tell the consultant. Sadly, I was clutching at straws. Paul's brain stem was alive but if he survived he would be disabled. I could not see my active son in that situation. So permission was given to withdraw the liquids that were keeping him alive.

When I got the phone call to say Paul had passed away, it set me on a journey. I had to arrange his funeral. I could not weep because if I started I would never stop. I took my dog for a walk up a hill and just screamed and screamed. I did weep at Paul's funeral but can't recall much as I had been given medication to help me. I knew the church was packed with many of Pauls friends. No-one had a bad word to say about him.

I was sixty four years old and left with the question - what now?

I knew if I stayed at home I would just wallow in my own pity and I wouldn't be able to go on. I began a cleaning business. Slowly I accepted what had happened and the anger I had felt began to subside.

My anger was eased as I began to have dreams of Paul in which we talked. Other strange things began to happen, the phone would ring twice and stop. Then one night as I lay in bed I heard three knocks on the window. My bedroom is on an upper floor. I knew it was Paul's way of letting me know he was well. It has been twelve long years since Paul passed and I still get what I call 'visitations' and I can sense his presence when I am sitting alone at night."

Irene Winton Tayside

I had met Irene in my capacity as a Spirit medium after she contacted me to ask for a reading. Her son, Paul, communicated very clearly with his Mother. It became apparent that Paul had been into bodybuilding and had taken a legal substance which had caused a terrible reaction within his body. Paul wanted his mother to know he had taken the substance of his own volition but had no idea it would harm him. He did not commit suicide.

It is apparent from Irene's description of events that grief had threatened to consume her and several of the symptoms of grief were felt by her almost immediately after hearing of her son's condition and subsequently, after his passing.

She chose to work in order to get her through the darkness and trauma of her loss. Irene had a strong conviction of life after death and was comforted in her belief that her son Paul was communicating to her through her dreams and was ever close to her when she was alone at home. It would seem that such a belief had helped Irene to cope with the grief in her own way. Her son Paul brought her the very important message from Spirit that he had not committed suicide and that she was right to state he would not have done such a thing

.As much as Irene was comforted by a message from Spirit, not everyone has such faith or belief.

I am often guided by my Spirit guides and given words of wisdom especially when I ask about death and life beyond. The following are words from one of my Spirit guides, Chang-Li.

"*Like the leaf on a tree clinging desperately to its branch, defying the onset of winter by holding on for all its worth. This image echoes the last Spring of life as we watch the battle being bravely fought by a loved one, deeply drawn into the breath that is slowly retreating, eager to stop and give passage to the Spirit of life, encumbered within a failing body. To observe closely this truth is to witness the miracle of death, dear ones. Just as the miracle of birth brings forward new life, so too does death manifest the entrance to life eternal. 'Tis but a journey home to freedom from earthly burdens and pains. Never fear, dear ones, the journey is laid before all. To seek comfort in grief is no small task, but we provide our knowledge in these words that all may come to an understanding that life and death can never be separated. Live now dear ones, in faith, in trust, in the wisdom of one who wishes only that you be loved in life as you are in death."*

Blessings to you Chang-Li

Mediumship often gets a bad press with mediums being criticized and accused of raising the dead or not letting the dead rest in peace. I can only speak from my own experiences as a medium and the reward for me is not monetary but emotional. Seeing the change in a person's grief-stricken face as I give a message from their loved one is reward enough for me. Just to let them know their loved one is safe and more alive than ever and all they want is for the living to go on living. I have been fortunate enough to have received grateful thanks from many people who have stated their life has changed and that they can go on living knowing that one day, they will be re-united with their loved one, which includes much loved animals.

When the death of a person is due to the criminal act of another, the anger felt by family and friends is often increased and emotions turn to thoughts of revenge. The need to find closure through justice is strong. Grief plays an intense part in the life of those left behind to grieve. What we need to realise is that grief is the fuel that powers the motive of relatives and friends who only desire to bring to justice the guilty party who chose to take the life of their loved one. That grief is compounded when the perpetrator is known to the deceased and their family. It can destroy normal family relations. Many people never get over such a tragedy and no longer take part in life, excluding and isolating themselves from society. How this saddens those in spirit. Working regularly with Spirit I hear and feel the hurt from the Spirit messenger when they try to bring comfort to the receiver of their message.

I have no easy answers to provide, only that I feel their presence and know they are well in Spirit. Trying to convey this can be quite distressing and any medium will know that it takes its toll on all involved.

There are times when a death is so unexpected and traumatic for the family, that they find themselves unable to actually speak the words of how it happened. The cause of death has been so hard to believe that saying how it happened is not possible. This usually happens when a death is by suicide, where the family and friends have had no idea that the deceased was even considering ending their life.

There are so many questions that run through the minds of those left to grieve. Then there is the guilt at not seeing the signs and the wondering if they could have prevented the death by being more attentive to the deceased.

All these thoughts and questions can be debilitating to those left behind. Grief threatens to drain the ability to live from their veins. Hearts are so broken that it feels they will never mend and may I say, they often never mend completely.

If we look also at the death of a baby who has died in the womb, the sense of loss for the mother and all who waited with excitement for the birth, cannot be measured. The pain of loss crushes the breath from the parents, leaving such a void that nothing brings comfort. In the absence of a little body to bury, the parents are left with more hurt, which leaves them thinking - did I do something to cause the death? And - where will my baby be?

. . .

My work as a medium has seen me give profound messages to parents who have lost a child. I recall here one message to a mother who lost a son in the early stages of pregnancy. This lady had mourned for so long and had blamed herself for the loss of her baby for many years. The message from her child came in the year when her son would have reached his twenty first birthday. This lady's son asked me to explain to his Mum that he was never meant to live, that he had only to experience the presence in her womb, before returning to the Spirit world where he could progress further into higher realms. He wanted to thank his Mum for the wonderful opportunity she gave him. At the time I found it hard to believe and wondered did I say something too far-fetched to believe. Yet sometime later, I discovered that what this young man had told me was, in fact, correct. This young man's mother kindly gave me permission to tell her story which is told in full in my first book, *No Proof Required.*

The answers to so many questions are difficult to define. In general, people see things differently and one answer to the same question may not bring the peace that is needed. Moving forward from loss is a personal journey that no-one can take for you. Each person will find their own way to recover sufficiently to carry on living some sort of normal life. When families are dealing with loss, parents and siblings may find it hard to express how they are feeling or are maybe frightened to say something that may cause distress to another family member.

There are no easy answers and no guidelines to follow in the hope emotions will settle. Psychologists, psychotherapists and grief counsellors can offer some helpful ways to overcome grief. They can assist by helping the grieving person to use methods and tools to help when they become angry, sad, depressed or suicidal.

The stages of grief don't always roll in order:

Denial, Anger, Blame, Depression, Acceptance.

I believe that there are many more symptoms and stages of grief. Each one may be particular to any one person.

If we think of the family left behind to grieve for a son or daughter who has been murdered and the body never found, how palpable is the grief that is compounded by the sense of injustice. It is then that grief compels the need for justice. This need becomes a way of life which takes over and develops into a purpose that is so strong that even the person searching and seeking answers is unaware of its influence, to the point that it smothers any other form of living. Many times, families have been torn apart because one member is so intent on finding justice for the deceased that other members become isolated and feel ignored or no longer a crucial part of the family. Life and breath are slowly drained from those who grieve. Often their physical being becomes sick and unhealthy, as if the life was sucked from them when their loved one died.

Murder is an act so brutal and final that nothing can bring a sense of peace to those left behind. When the perpetrator refuses to divulge the whereabouts of the body this adds more pain and anxiety to the relatives. The need to provide a fitting end in the form of a burial or cremation, which allows people to say a final farewell, is robbed from them. The unanswered questions and the feeling of helplessness can drive a person to distraction. The endless nightmares and terrible thoughts which invade the lives of those who grieve brings no mercy, especially if they do not know how or where their loved one perished, Truly a living nightmare.

I am a mother and grandmother and I have often worried when my daughter or granddaughters are away from home, especially at night. Our world seems to be ever changing and the respect for life is diminishing. This causes any parent or partner to feel anxious if their loved one is late home or stays out without any contact to say where they are. It is natural to become fearful for their safety.

I am aware of mediums who have clear premonitions of disasters or tragedies that have unfolded just as they have seen. To try to prevent these things from happening is not an easy task, as often mediums are classed as cranks or just seeking publicity. Some people who have no inclination of Spiritual or psychic abilities have experienced these premonitions and can find themselves troubled and desperate to help, only to find there is nothing they can do stop the event from happening. It is especially difficult if the premonition or dream involves a family member.

ALLESSANDRA'S STORY

The following story from a lady tells of her premonition before the death of her Father. She explains how vividly she saw a funeral with the coffin, the pallbearers and all the colours she saw.

. . .

"My Dad died in his early eighties, very peacefully in hospital surrounded by all his family. I was not unprepared for his death as the week previously I had experienced a premonition. It was so vivid - I could see the coffin, the pallbearers, the colours of the flowers, yellow, white, purple and blue. It was strange and I thought to myself, "I don't know anyone who is going to die". A few days after this premonition I received a telephone call from my mother to say Dad was unwell and she had called an ambulance. The next call came from my sister to say Dad was failing fast and to get to the hospital quickly. He died of heart failure and leukaemia. Another strange thing happened as his funeral was being arranged. We were at my parents' home when suddenly a brilliant ray of light flooded into the lounge and a wonderful sense of happiness filled the room. I felt Dad was there overseeing his funeral arrangements. His whole source of life had been happiness, he loved life, was a born entertainer, the life and soul of a party. I kept myself busy with work and found myself retuning to my music and immersing myself in song. It was my mother who gave me the strength to carry on. I was aware of her determination that life has to go on.

It took years to recover and my outlook on life changed dramatically. I now acknowledge that our life on earth has a definite purpose. I always thought that my purpose was to be a classical singer, but when obstacles seemed to be put in my way, I followed a new path, a Spiritual one. I became a healer and holistic therapist. I feel that we are in this physical life for a period of time and when our time is over, we leave our physical body behind and return home (the etheric world). I developed an interest in past lives as I believe we live many lives. I know there are many questions to be answered. I am still developing my interest in past lives and have qualified as a past life regressionist."

Allessandra Pritchard

Essex.

As you see by Allessandra's story, her life changed dramatically through experiencing the death of her father. She is a wonderful classical singer but continues to work in the field of holistic therapies.

Many people may doubt the existence of a Spirit world where life continues after physical death. Yet we will all experience the journey home after our body has ceased to function.

As a medium I am aware that the Spirit world consists of many levels, just as it states in the Bible, "In my Father's house there are many mansions". For me, this confirms the truth and helps me explain to someone who is grieving the loss of a loved one who had their life ended by the reckless conduct of another. When such a person who is deemed to be wicked, dies, they too find themselves in the Spirit world. However, the level that they enter is far different from that of someone who has lived a decent life.

My Spirit guide tells me that we all enter the Spirit world and depending on our actions and life on Earth, we will find ourselves in the appropriate level. However, all have the opportunity to advance to higher levels or to atone for behaviour that is considered bad, wicked or unkind.

Many times, I hear the fears of someone who is grieving, who worries that their loved one will be in limbo, floating around endlessly in the cosmos. Usually they say that their loved one did not believe in life after death, so they ask - "Where will they be?" I hope I explain in a way that calms their fears and allows them to accept that their loved one will be safe and looked after by those who have gone before. The connection is always about Love. The Spirit world has many intelligent beings who are there to help and assist those who return. No-one is left alone. Even much-loved pets are welcomed home when they die.

The common theme that runs through these stories is the action taken by most of the people who were grieving. That action was to throw themselves into work. I always feel this is just a distraction and it invariably acts as a means to an end in that it detracts the constant thoughts of the deceased. It provides a respite from the grief, but it does not bring lasting comfort. There are other ways to overcome grief to allow sanity to return. One such way is to seek the help of a grief counsellor. This is a good way to start as grief counsellors are specially trained to help. One method they use is to encourage the person to speak about their relative who has died. It is also helpful in distinguishing grief from trauma. When a person is grieving they often focus on the image of their relative as they were when they died and find it extremely hard to get any destructive images from their mind. They are traumatised by the image. This leads to lack of sleep, an inability to concentrate, exhaustion and finally physical illness. Grief counsellors can help the person to focus not on the end of their loved ones' life but on the memories and phases of their life, the good times, their achievements. Another action that can be taken and is found to be very useful, is to hold a memorial or celebration of the deceased's' life.

Writing a letter to the loved one and saying all that was felt and not expressed before the death is a way of releasing guilt. As a medium, I have heard many times the sorrowful tale of a relative who feels they should have told their loved one how much they were loved and appreciated. The same goes for a spirit communicator who comes forward with the message of sadness that they failed to acknowledge their love to family while in the physical life.

I recall my own difficulty after my father's death; the guilt I felt at the last words spoken in anger. It took me a long time to come to terms with my actions. My father had struggled with alcoholism for a long time which escalated after my mother died. I tried desperately to help him. The last week of his life I had worked hard clearing and cleaning his flat. I threw out many empty alcohol bottles. He had been in hospital after collapsing and this helped him to virtually dry out. My sister and I hoped he had turned a corner and would get his life back on track. Sadly, this did not happen. Just a week later he was found dead behind the living room door by his friend. He had used alcohol to drink himself into oblivion. The one good thing to come from this was his friend's shock at finding him. His friend was also an alcoholic and had been disowned by his family. The shock took its toll but brought his friend to his senses. He stopped drinking and re-engaged with his family. At least some good came from my father's death.

Following the advice from a grief counsellor, I found it helped to talk about Dad and recall the good memories. A father is an instrumental person in a child's life and losing a father can be distressing and traumatic. The relationship between a father and daughter is often filled with tenderness and a strong sense of being indestructible. It is essential that we realise our life is of a human nature and as such, we will suffer the gamut of emotions that can overwhelm us during these times. It may not be the death of a person but of a much-loved animal. The emotions will be similar and just as traumatic.

. . .

This next story is from a lady who had to deal with the death of her beloved pet dog, Penny. Having an animal in your life is so rewarding and comforting. They give unconditional love without the need for any form of recompense. They sense when we are sad and happy. All they want is to be loved and cared for and have a warm bed, food and toys if the need is there. They come into our lives to enrich them and there are times when their company is all we need to get us through difficult times. Their loss is harder to bear when they have been with their owner for many years, since they were young. Grief is strong and their absence is felt just as intensely as the loss of a loved one.

PENNY THE BORDER TERRIER

Penny, our Border terrier died at thirteen years of age from cancer. Penny was just a small puppy when she came to us. At first I wanted nothing to do with her, but dogs have a way of getting under your skin. We got another Border terrier and I felt Penny was being left out. I began to feed her and pay special attention to her. When Penny became ill we took her to the vet who gave her some medication which worked for a while. She became more poorly and we returned to the vet. It was established that Penny had a mass in her abdomen but the vet could not tell what it was. The vet said it could be a cyst but an operation would help to find out exactly what it was. We gave permission for the operation, but said if the mass was a problem and things were too bad just to allow Penny to die. We did not want her woken up after the operation if she would need to be euthanized at a later date. I tried to keep my hopes up as we waited for news. At lunchtime, my husband told me Penny had not made it. At that moment, time just stood still. I could not believe she had gone.

Over the weeks she was ill I had spoken to her, telling her it was alright to go and to return home. Penny's death has left a huge hole in my heart, and the feelings are so raw. I found it hard to speak without becoming emotional. I do have the comfort of knowing she is no longer in pain but I still feel her around me. Penny would put her nose in my hand which was her way of saying she wanted to be petted. I felt her presence one night at my bedside and felt her nose in my hand. It's less than a year since Penny died and I still struggle to cope. Penny was part of our family and was just as important as the humans. Our other dog looks everywhere for her. He refuses to lie on the dog bed and often sits and stares at the place where Penny would sit. He will not go near the area where we buried Penny but looks from a distance.

My belief in the Spirit world helps me as I know animals survive in Spirit as well as humans and I will see her again."

Anonymous Cupar

It was sad to hear of Penny's passing. Weeks earlier I had called at her owner's home for another reason. Her owner had told me she was ill, but her husband was not ready to let her go. I was sitting in the conservatory talking with the owner's friend when Penny came and sat beside me. She looked straight at me and I could feel her emotion. Penny was telepathically telling me she was ready to go and wanted me to tell her owner. I responded to Penny telepathically, saying I would try. Penny then left my side. As I was leaving the house, I took the owner aside and told her what had occurred with Penny. She accepted this but was unsure if she should tell her husband because he was so attached to Penny and was clearly unable to let her go.

I can understand where people will think it is impossible to communicate with a dog, but I have often given information through a Spirit message by means of pictures in my mind that come from the presence of an animal in Spirit. There are of course many people who can communicate with the animals and the messages these animals bring have a profound effect on the owners that helps to heal their grief.

REMEMBERING

As I write this paragraph, my own heart breaks after losing my beautiful pet rabbit CoCo. I had her since she was eight weeks old. She was small and completely black. CoCo brought me many happy memories and taught me how to love an animal unconditionally. She had a very independent spirit and made sure I and my family knew it. The only time she ever spent in a hutch was when I was away from home and she spent some time in a small animal kennels. Even the lady owner observed CoCo's independent streak. Despite trying to find her a rabbit friend she just wouldn't mix with other rabbits. She was nine years and one week old when she died. It seemed to be pneumonia as she was struggling to breathe. The vet tried as best he could but she didn't respond to the medication. I tried using my Colour Therapy Lights to help her breathe more easily. The colour Orange was too strong for her and I changed it to Turquoise which seemed to help. However, as her breathing became more difficult, she would not lie under the light. I was due to take her to the vet at 9.10 a.m. the following day but she took a turn for the worse at 7.30 a.m. and passed away. I had spent the night lying on the floor beside her to keep her warm. As a family we felt it was better to bury her in the garden as she loved to roam in her garden. I can say without a shred of doubt that my grief was palpable and I cried hard for my beautiful fur baby. The first week after her death, I slept very fitfully and found it hard to sit in the conservatory looking at her cage and toys. I know it will be a long time before I can feel comfortable in the conservatory without looking at the place where she would stretch out and sleep.

So you see, the loss of a pet has a profound effect just as much as losing a loved one. Grief strikes at the most inconvenient times, and often tears fall and a heart breaks a little more. I and my family created a little memorial in our back garden which was a big help to me in accepting CoCo was gone. As a medium I know she will have crossed the rainbow bridge and be among other animals and I'm sure my family in Spirit will take care of her. As silly as it seems, I sent my thoughts out to the world of Spirit to give me a sign that she was safe and well. My daughter had two dreams in which she saw CoCo in our garden, happy and healthy. The day after I sent my thoughts up to Spirit I got my sign. It came as I entered a shop, one I would never have thought of entering, and found a lovely rabbit shaped badge with the words "Crazy Rabbit Lady". It was on a table with sale items. It was the only one, and of course I bought it.

Creating a memorial for CoCo was instrumental in my accepting her death. I had been unable to let her body be taken out of the conservatory. I wanted to keep her close for as long as I could. The little funeral we held allowed me to let go of her little body. My family had another animal, a cat called Lola. CoCo and Lola had come to accept each other but were never friendly. They just put up with each other and would stand nose to nose. If Lola strayed too close to CoCo in her cage, she soon found out how grumpy CoCo could be. I thought it best to let Lola see CoCo's dead body, in order that she understood why

Coco was no longer in our house. My heart ached as I watched Lola sniff CoCo all over, then lick her face before walking away.

It's almost seven weeks since CoCo rabbit crossed the rainbow bridge. I still find myself thinking of the morning she died. Tears run down my face as I recall her last moments. I steal myself to think of the happy times and the mischief she got up to. A memory comes to mind of how she would steal my youngest granddaughter's toast. One morning, I was in the kitchen after giving Abbey her plate of toast cut up into triangles. She was sitting on the living room floor watching TV. Suddenly I heard her shout "That's my toast CoCo!" Then I saw CoCo running into the hall with a triangle of toast in her mouth, pursued by Abbey, who quickly grabbed the toast from CoCo and began to eat it. Not a single thought of germs entered her head. It was funny. Poor CoCo followed her back to the living room, begging for another piece of toast.

It's so easy to think when our pets die, they are not as important as when a relative or friend dies. Our pets and animals are a source of comfort and give so much love and joy, they deserve our respect and to be cared for and cherished.

I have found it hard to part with CoCo's toys and blankets. I keep her little brass bell on display and recall how she would lift it and make it ring or if she was in a strop she would lift it and throw it about. She was such a character. I miss her so much. When I sit in the conservatory I look at the place where she would lie, stretched out and chilled. I try to smile but once more tears fall. But through my work with Spirit I am so aware that she will be alright in the Spirit realms.

This may be hard for others to comprehend and when they lose someone, people often feel that there is nothing of their loved one left. Quite often I hear people say "When you're dead your dead". How sad I feel for them. If they could only grasp the fact that life is eternal and the Soul or the true essence of the person has gone on to a new and exciting journey.

My Spirit guide Chang-Li gave me these words of wisdom:

"We should not fear Death for just as Life is a gift for your world, so too is Death a gift for ours. Life in all its forms is precious and Death brings that preciousness back to the Etheric. The Etheric is all existence. It is all around you and within you, whether you exist in your world or ours. All are one. Nothing is separate. As you evolve in your physical form, so too does your very soul evolve in the Etheric world, as within, so without.
Death does not separate, it confirms the oneness of all.
Do not fear Death for through Death, Life gains Immortality."

Blessings to you Chang-Li

I understand that many people will find these words hard to accept and may think it is a figment of my imagination. However, having served the Spirit world for many years, I have complete faith in my guides. I know they share words of wisdom with me in order that I may have the courage and strength to continue to work as I do. I know for certain that my guides would not give me these words if they were not helpful to mankind.

Some readings that I have given in my capacity as a medium have turned out to be more of a form of counselling. Many people have said they have felt better for just talking to someone who doesn't judge or think that they are being dramatic. I try to listen rather than talk when a reading takes this track.

However, there are several methods which I have suggested to some people: for instance, encouraging the person to get creative, even if it's just writing about their feelings. This can help in releasing pent up emotions and can allow the person to write words they find difficult to speak. Being creative is a way to accept the death in a better way. To write the story of a loved one or pet can assist in the healing process by recalling the happier times and memories rather than focusing on the last days; or creating a collage of pictures and stories of their loved one depicting the times of laughter and joy.

Memorials are also a good way to remember a pet or loved one. Especially if the death resulted in the failure to find a body. This is extremely difficult to deal with and the memorial provides a way in which goodbyes can be expressed. Finding a favourite place to create the memorial helps in knowing you have been present at a place where your loved one was happy.

It takes a lot of time and effort to find the right way to remember a loved one. The memory of the last days or the last time someone was with or saw their loved one continually invades their mind, sometimes to the point of distraction. Their ability to think clearly is crippled by the thought of the death. In the case of a particularly tragic death it is even harder to escape from the memory or the thoughts of how their loved one suffered. That is why it is important to find a right way of remembering. People feel that to talk about the death with someone would bring up the bad memories, when in fact talking about the loved one is a way to recall the good times. Recalling their characters and quirky ways that made you laugh or smile helps to keep them alive in a good way.

On many occasions when giving a reading, I have been asked, "Are they alright?" or "Did they suffer?" My knowledge of the Spirit world helps me explain that they are alright and are more alive than ever. All they want is for their family, friends and colleagues to know that they still exist, albeit on another level of consciousness. The communicator from Spirit asks me to tell them that life goes on for them and should do for those left behind. Many will urge their families to go on living and not to have regrets. Quite often a communicator will tell me they regretted not telling their loved one how much they did love them or that they should have given more time to them. You see, in a way, they are trying to say Love now, not when it is too late.

The next story is from a lady and it tells of how she initially felt denial at her father's death. Denial is a mechanism that seems to be helpful but in fact it is obstructive in coming to terms with the passing of a loved one. She writes of her feeling of anger at having to share her precious moments with others at her father's funeral.

JOANNE'S STORY

"My father had cancer and passed away in hospital. On the morning my father passed, a few hours before his final earth-bound breath, I was sleeping but at approximately 3.a.m I woke as I heard my father say the words "It's my time". My father had come to tell me it was time for him to prepare to take his next steps. I gave him my blessing. I was frantic and distressed. This was the hardest thing I have ever had to do. I felt as if someone had reached into my chest and torn my heart out. Somehow, I fell back to sleep, probably from exhaustion and distress. Although we knew the time was approaching, when the phone rang a few hours later to say that we should go to the hospital as quickly as possible, my rational mind kicked in and as it was early morning, we reached the hospital quickly and took the lift to the ward. As soon as the lift doors opened my initial instinct was to run to him. As I stepped out into the corridor to the ward, I stopped and felt a chill. My father had taken his next steps. In that moment I had lost my beloved father, best friend and mentor.

Although I know we may not be physically together, we will never be apart. This gave comfort at this time. Nothing prepares you for this experience. In the hours and days that followed I felt as if I was in a parallel fog – in denial that this could have happened but having to function to ensure all formalities were completed. It is so difficult to put these first few weeks into words. I saw signs that my father was with me. Beautiful flowers, a stroke on the cheek, a presence around me, somehow giving me strength to continue.

I found it incredibly difficult to attend the funeral. I was so angry that I had to share such precious moments with others. I wanted this to be private but I knew this would not have been my father's wish. Now, nearly two years later, there are moments of laughter when we remember things that were done and said on the day.

However, on the day itself I was numb.

People rally round in those first few weeks with well-meaning intentions but quickly all have to go back to their own lives and suddenly you feel alone. This is when the real struggle begins, as the life you knew no longer exists and you have to find a way of being. There is no manual for this. People say well-meaning things but often this causes hurt as it can be misplaced; for example "You'll get over it". I don't believe we get over it. We merely find a way to live with it. Grief does not have a time limit. Perhaps the most surprising reaction of others is when they avoid you. They don't know what to say or do so they just avoid you, which is incredibly hurtful.

. . .

Not a day goes by that my father is not with me and most days I still cry with the pain of losing him from this physical world. I miss the simple things like a cup of coffee and a chat, a shared joke, listening to him whistling around the garden. Mostly I miss just being with him. These moments were precious. After my father passed it took a good three months before I began to see light at the end of the tunnel. I mean a little bit of strength was coming back. I was getting ready to start the healing process. My father's passing changed me as a person - my outlook on life and death absolutely changed. Death is the most cruel way to learn the lesson in life that we should not "sweat the small stuff" and that the "material" stuff" is not important. In life we should make memories every single day, as you don't know when the day will come that you will not be able to make more memories together.

If I have one piece of advice it would be to listen to your heart and soul. Take things day by day. Initially the days will be a struggle as you try to make sense of what is happening and find the strength to get up and face the world. In your own time, days will become a little less painful. This will never go away but you will find a way to deal with life differently. Expect triggers from the most unexpected places, a laugh, a smell, a song. These can stop you in your tracks. Most importantly never apologise for grieving. Do what you need to do to put one foot in front of the other, day by day. Don't feel guilty if you want to laugh or enjoy a movie. Seek help if you need to and take your own personal space and time to heal."

J Jones, Armadale

I could feel the sadness and hurt as I read this lady's story, yet her strength and her love for her father was evident with every word. The signs she received from her father were testament to the bond of everlasting love between them.

Many people may say the signs she felt were just her grief and wishful thinking to know her father was still in some way with her. Let me tell you, these signs are real and our loved ones who have passed on to the realms of Spirit work hard and with so much love, to bring us confirmation that their soul or consciousness (which ever you wish to call it) lives on. Their love, just as our love, goes on and never dies. This lady's story is heartfelt and inspiring.

LESSONS

There are many theories and suggestions as to what knowledge we have when we are born. Some say that we are here to learn and grow in order that we will progress in the Spirit world when we return. Others say that before we are born, our soul knows or chooses the life we will live, including the bad with the good. I find this a bit hard to swallow, especially if I see someone locked in a body that cannot function properly or communicate in any way. I do understand where the lessons from such a life would benefit those who love and care for such a person. As hard as it seems, such a life is worthwhile regardless of the pain it may bring both for the person and the carer.

Death brings so many lessons for every single person or animal who is touched by the passing. I, like so many others, have lost someone I loved and cherished through death. The lessons have been hard but essential to my growth and understanding of loss. So how do we overcome the physical, emotional, mental and Spiritual symptoms that threaten our sanity and leave us feeling bereft, losing hope and unable to function normally? There is no easy answer to that as each person reacts completely differently to such situations.

I have found that when a loved one is facing their mortality - someone who is suffering from a terminal illness and know they have reached the stage of life when death is approaching - they are often the one who teaches us the lesson. They are the one who will be passing through darkness to light, leaving their physical body which has become the darkness to be clothed in the light body which carries them safely to the etheric world, releasing any pain or suffering that they may have endured. As a medium I try to explain to people who have requested a reading that, as we are birthed into this life, so too are we once again birthed into the Spirit realms. Rather than thinking of the anniversary of the death, I ask them to consider celebrating their birthday in Spirit. As I write this section, I am wishing my mother a happy thirty ninth birthday in Spirit. This may seem silly to some but knowing my Mother is alive and well in Spirit helps me to remember her with joy rather than remembering the day she died. This is the same for my father, other relatives and friends and my pets who all now exist in Spirit.

The process of watching a loved one become weaker and weaker, dying in front of you while you feel helpless, can leave a body overwhelmed with guilt and traumatised to the extent that they begin to suffer physically and mentally. Knowing there are counsellors and people who are there to help is a bonus but getting someone to accept help or admit they need help is another matter altogether. As we will see in some of the stories, so many people throw themselves into work in a bid to recover some normality or to forget any harrowing memories. Although this may be helpful it only serves to put the problem on the back burner. Is it not better to express our emotions and release the tears and hurt rather than suppress them until physical illness occurs? Easier said than done, I hear you say. Yes, I agree. Yet it is the relatives, friends and colleagues or pets who have the ability to encourage us to seek help. This is why we, as people, need a better method of supporting not just someone who is grieving but to help ourselves when we are in such a position. Death is something that should not be whispered about but spoken of freely, not treated as a bad thing but just the progression from this life to the next eternal life. I know this sounds easy for me as a medium and believer in life after death but how much better would it be if we all had this knowledge. This may not suit every religious leader but it certainly would allow people to think differently and to react positively to death rather than find themselves tortured with grief.

I do not mean to sound as if I am preaching. All I want to do is give those who grieve another option to help them deal with a death and move forward with hope, knowing that a time will come when they will be reunited with their loved one or pet.

I recall here an occasion when I gave a message from Spirit to a young man from his grandmother. This young man had been very close to her and found it difficult to continue living without her in his life. His grandmother made it very clear in her message to him that she was still in his life and was aware of how he was feeling. She encouraged him to continue doing his job which he loved and for which she had given him a good grounding, She, had supported him by passing her own knowledge of the work whilst she had lived with him. She told him of many things that were occurring in his life and that she would always watch over him. This gave this young man the jolt he needed to begin to move on with his life. A simple reading with a simple message that had such a huge impact. So, you see, death does not separate us from those we love.

Finding ways to cope with grief can be a strenuous task. Many people need time and space to work through their emotions and sometimes people act out of character. The mind and brain seem to struggle to focus on what is necessary and instead focus on random things that are unsuitable and frustrating. Many people, including myself, have found themselves standing in the street or supermarket wondering why they are there or what they are supposed to be doing. Time and time again they shed tears and become distressed knowing full well that they must find a way to live and breathe and continue with work, and life in general. I found it hard to face my colleagues when I returned to work after my mother's death. My colleagues were unsure of what to say to me and when they did pass their condolences, I just burst into tears. Sleep was practically impossible as the memory of the day kept resurfacing in my mind. You are on automatic pilot for so long before some form of sanity prevails and the light at the end of the tunnel appears. It may be still some distance away but at least there is progress. As time goes on the next step is to deal with the first anniversary. That brings new concerns as you realise a year has passed. Guilt creeps in and the thought that you got through a year without your loved one makes you feel that you were forgetting about them. I have said already that, as a medium, I try to help people and say that I look at the anniversaries as birthdays in Spirit. I know the Spirit world celebrates the arrival of someone who has passed through death into eternal life. It is a welcome home party and many family and friends are there to greet the journeyer. My Spirit guides, when discussing a death, would always call the deceased "the journeyer". I was told that death is the final journey home. I ask my guides to help me understand the process that occurs when someone has made their transition to Spirit. Sometimes the answers I get puzzle me but they always ensure I can relay these answers to others in a simple and compassionate manner.

The question of suicide comes up a lot when I work as a medium. It is hard to deal with when someone stands before me with tears in their eyes and states "Why did they do it?" or "Why did I not see or recognise the signs?" There is so much blame, guilt and even self-criticism attached to such a passing. The one thing I do my best to explain is that when someone has made the decision to end their life, nothing or no-one will prevent the inevitable. I choose my words carefully as I wish to convey the message from their loved one as honestly and compassionately as I can. May people who have ended their life through suicide will ask me to tell their loved one how sorry they are to have caused such distress and hurt. However, they do wish their loved one to know that they are now at peace. This is the same for the relative who is grieving; they too wish to apologise as they feel that they have somehow let the deceased down by not being there at their time of need. The worst situation for me is when the grieving person belongs to a religion where suicide is considered a sin and the deceased is in limbo or purgatory. For any medium this is difficult to persuade the grieving person that purgatory does not exist within the Spirit realms and that everyone is met and welcomed home. No one, no matter how good or bad they have been in the physical world is left in limbo or left to rot in some undesirable universe. Everyone enters the realms of Spirit, whether they believe it exists or not. Many are familiar with the saying in the Bible. The phrase "In my Father's house there are many mansions" pertains to the levels within the Spirit world. Each person who passes to Spirit has the opportunity to evolve and grow which allows them the opportunity to progress. It would be hard to swallow if it was felt someone who was of a despicable and nasty nature, who had committed dreadful crimes, would be welcomed to the same level as someone who had lived a gracious and honourable life. Yet even people who are wicked have the opportunity to atone for their actions and to progress to a higher level.

When we consider our animal friends, they too survive the condition called death. They cross what mediums call "the rainbow bridge". What excitement is felt when an owner is once again reunited with their dog, cat, rabbit or any other pet. The joy is indescribable, so I am told. Having given messages from some pets to a grieving owner, I see the happiness in their faces as they realise that the animal is still wagging its tail, purring, hopping, flying, running around full of energy and fun. Now don't get me wrong - I am not someone who can speak "animal". What I get is the image of the animal and then I see pictures that are being conveyed to me through mind to mind. Some animals are very good at letting me see images of the owners and their homes. Many times, a dog has shown me its favourite toy which is often the proof the owner needs to know their animal is communicating. I find such messages very satisfying as there are times when an animal has been the owner's only companion for many years. The grief felt is just as unbearable and hard to deal with. This is one reason why telling an owner "It's just a dog (animal)" can be very detrimental to the process of recovering from the loss.

Animals love unconditionally.

I have already written of ways to help the process of recovery, such as memorials and keeping a lock of hair or a cutting of fur. There are websites with people who create beautiful pieces of jewellery that can hold the lock of hair or fur. This is a wonderful way to feel the closeness of our loved ones now in Spirit.

Many things in life happen to teach us lessons. Situations occur that test our commitment and our reserve. As I write this section, I and many around the world, are trying to come to terms with the loss of life through a pandemic. This virus that has spread rapidly across countries all over the world is named COVID – 19; a pneumonia type illness that is killing so many elderly, infirm and those with serious underlying conditions. It has taken its toll on many medical staff who are battling to prevent the spread and to keep people alive. We are being urged to sit up and take stock. To look at what is important in life and what changes need to be made. This pandemic has resulted in a situation called lockdown. People are being told to self-isolate. Relatives of the ill and dying are unable to be at their side. Funerals can only be attended by five to ten people. This tragedy is creating a sense of dis-association, taking away the human touch which heals so many conditions and emotions. I cannot help but feel extremely sad at the terrible consequences of this pandemic and the effects it is causing and will continue to cause long after the virus has been eradicated.

Grief, has the ability to instil debilitating and destructive thoughts which can bring us to our knees and prevent us from living contentedly. In this present stage, as the virus is being fought, I fear for the vulnerable and those who live alone. People need people, they need pets. A simple touch of a hand, a smile or a wagging tail can do wonders to cheer a soul and encourage them to move forward. My own thoughts are that grief will be exaggerated in so many ways. Mental health will suffer in those who were ill or those who lost a loved one to the virus. There will be intolerable suffering by those who were unable to be by the side of their loved ones as they drew their last breath. The separation and restrictions imposed will leave many questions that will likely never be answered. These devastating conditions will see people become withdrawn, emotionally and mentally unstable, feel totally unable to change their thoughts and even feel suicidal. The knowing that a loved one died alone can cause such misery and hurt. Being unable to say a last goodbye and tell someone how much they meant and were loved can store up sad memories that will be present for a long time and even creep into thoughts at a happier time. Getting through the darkness to light will be no easy task.

It is in our grief we tend to call out to God or some other deity demanding to know why a death has occurred and why it was allowed to happen. It is not easy to answer when the question is put to me. I am aware that not everyone will choose to believe that life continues after death. If I can in some way plant the seed that allows a grieving relative to explore this concept and begin to realise that their loved one is safe and living in a higher vibrational level, then at least some good may come from my Spirit messages.

We must be aware that our loved ones in Spirit draw so close to us at times of sorrow. They want us to know that as each person or animal passes to Spirit they are not alone. The one who has left their earthly body is assisted in their transition by those in Spirit who are there to welcome them home. I know this may be some small comfort but to have the knowledge that our loved ones have gone before and God has not abandoned us, is a step towards healing our grief.

As hard as it is to accept, those in the Spirit world are aware of many tragedies. Think of the past wars and conflicts where so many died. The thought of the Spirit world being aware and able to help so many through the darkness is humbling. Yes, they too must suffer at such needless loss of life, knowing that they cannot prevent such disasters. Man's inhumanity to man knows no boundaries. Violence solves nothing and through anger at a death, violent reactions will not relieve the symptoms of grief.

One thing I do know from conversations with my Spirit guides is that life must go on. The need to learn from such difficult lessons is paramount to one's survival. We are Souls within a physical body and our Soul needs to learn in order to progress, not just in the physical world, but within the realms of Spirit when we return home. Life and Death cannot be separated and those we love will be waiting until the day the grand re-union happens.

I have written about this pandemic and of course I have my own thoughts on how this occurred. I asked one of my Spirit guides the question "Was this virus released deliberately?" Here is the answer I received from my guide Chang-Li.

"Do not dwell on the cause but work diligently and carefully in eradicating the effects. Welcome the opportunity that has arisen for change. For too long now Earth has been ravaged and destroyed. Mankind has taken the mantle of power and brought catastrophe after catastrophe. Here is another man-made disaster that you must use to deliver a new way of living. A way that sees Man care for Man, that Man cares for all living beings. Man must care for Earth. Know this, Earth can exist without Man but Man cannot and will not exist without Earth."

    Blessings to you Chang-Li

. . .

I am grateful to have such a special bond with my Spirit guides and friends. The knowledge I have gained makes my life seem more precious. Death holds no fear for me. Like many people it is not death that scares them but HOW THEY WILL DIE. When we lose someone we love to an accident or through a crime, we put ourselves through hell trying to think about how bad it must have been, how they must have suffered and whether they called out the name of their relative or partner. It is such a horrendous time that grief is heightened and any sense of reality is squashed by these frightening thoughts. I try to bring comfort through my messages from Spirit. When a recipient of a message begins to cry tears of joy rather than sadness, it is a small reward for me. Many times, I have been really surprised by the information given from Spirit.

On one occasion I had to tell a father that his wee girl in Spirit had laughed at him as he hurt his finger while gardening. The father held his hand up to show me a sore finger. He smiled and confirmed that is exactly what his daughter would have done.

Another occasion saw me pass a message to a lady who had lost her beloved dog. Now as I have already said I do not speak dog or any animal language. This dog showed itself to me so clearly and I described it to the lady who began to cry. I then saw the image of a small pup of the same breed and told the lady. She said the small pup had only just been bought and was at home and the lady was feeling as if she had let her old dog down by getting a new pup. I was able to let her know that her old dog was happy and would play with the new pup. The lady was laughing and shouted "Oh My God! I do see the pup, she seems to be jumping at something, wagging her tail and barking happily but I can't see anything". I was able to tell her that her old dog was showing me images of the new pup which included the fact that one of its ears would always flop forward. She confirmed this was correct.

The Spirit world is all around us and those we love still care and watch over us. They even send signs that they are around. In times of quiet, when we are almost daydreaming, they will draw close. You may feel a breeze even though all windows and doors are closed. Maybe you suddenly smell the favourite scent of your Mum or a particular smell of cigars that your Dad always smoked. Children in Spirit will take great joy in making lights flicker or turning the TV off and on. They can be mischievous and hide things like car keys or mobile phones. These are all signs that Spirits are close by. Sometimes you may consistently hear the same song on the radio or television. A song that meant something to you and your loved one. I always say to just acknowledge them by saying "Hi" or "Ok I know you are here".

Spirits can be very helpful if we let them. When I lose something or forget where I put it, I call out to Spirit and soon a thought or image comes to me and I know where to find the item. On one occasion as I worked with some women in an office, one lady was upset as an item she posted had not been received. She called the recipient, who stated they had not received it. I heard her say when the item was posted, it was in an envelope supplied by the sender. As she finished the call, without thinking I blurted out, "It's in their mail room. Tell them to go check". She looked at me as if I had two heads. I just said, "You will get a call in around an hour's time to say they have found it". Sure enough the call came and the sender told her it was found in the mail room. The look on the lady's face was so funny. She demanded to know how I knew this. I had not told anyone in the office that I was a medium. I replied saying it was female intuition.

This happened another time but it was with my daughter. We were moving house and had everything loaded up in the removal van but still hadn't received the call from the solicitor to uplift the keys of the new house. My daughter was fretting and getting anxious. I said the call will come at noon to pick up the key. She wasn't convinced. Then at 11.59 a.m. the phone rang. I laughed and said "I told you!" Spirit said all would be well and it was. We moved into the new house and love it.

When we move house or country we think that we are leaving our Spirit friends behind, but let me say that is so wrong. Those in spirit are fully aware of any potential move and will be just as excited as we are. In fact, they probably reach the new destination before we do. Please do not think that you are deserting them, especially pets that you may have buried within your garden, like I have done with my beautiful Coco rabbit. Remember it's only their old broken or worn out body that is buried there. Their Soul is very much alive and free to follow you wherever you may go. This is why I try to convince people not to spend every day visiting a gravesite. It may bring comfort for a while but it will eventually become a habit- one that will continue to add to any grief that you already feel. Your loved one is not there and they do not want you to sit and cry at their grave. They want you to honour them by living. "Take the flowers home and enjoy them", is the message given from the deceased.

There is no right or wrong way to grieve. Just as there is no right or wrong way to pick up the pieces of a broken heart and carry on living. Each person is unique and how they recover will differ in so many ways to others. This next story tells of the destructive side of grief and the importance of having help from a professional and the advantages of channelling emotions into something positive. It is clear that grief, is debilitating. While some people can overcome their sadness and hurt to move on, others find comfort in other ways. You will see how turning to alcohol was this man's way of dealing with his grief. Many mediums and those who have a belief in the Spirit world will understand the part where the father found a way to help his son. Some may think it was just his imagination. I will leave the reader to decide.

JOHN'S STORY

"My father passed to Spirit in 1986. His death hit me hard and I found his passing extremely difficult to deal with. I turned to alcohol to ease the pain.

Up to that point I never took a drink until after 8pm, but as time went on I began to enter depression. My alcohol consumption began at 8.30 am after my children went to school and my wife had gone to the shopping centre. On one particular morning, I took down a new bottle of spirits and a beer. Looking at my father's photo and crying, I poured out a drink.

I spoke out loud, "Dad please help me. I am getting into serious trouble with alcohol". I lifted the glass and took a sip. It was the most horrible taste I have ever tasted. The beer had the exact same horrible taste. I knew the bottles had been untouched and looking again at Dad's photo I said, "Thank you Dad. I am so grateful to you". I went into the kitchen and poured the alcohol down the sink. I have never used alcohol since. My father was an alcoholic for many years of his short life and I absolutely believe that he did not want his son to end up the same way. My father had been in Spirit for two years when this happened. I can say that during the time I was grieving my father's passing, life held little or no value to me; in fact, the thought of joining him in Spirit was on my mind constantly. I had three wonderful children and I found it difficult to be a father to them. My wife was supportive at this time, but even that had little or no meaning for me. I just felt useless. My doctor referred me to a counsellor, whose name was Don and with his support I began to make sense of it all and started to make my life more positive. Many years later I ran an alcohol awareness programme and shared my story with many people and students. That lasted eleven years. It took a long time to deal with my grief but my father's help was vital to my survival."

John O'C, Galway

Death is not the end and those in Spirit will always have our best interest at heart. They will find ways to help us get life moving again. Is it not comforting to know that our loved ones are watching over us and still caring? John's story is heartwarming in that he eventually found a way to live again and to use his experience to help others.

It is not my plan to push people into believing in the Spirit world but how much more would this knowledge be of benefit to those who find their life at a standstill?

I have listened to people as they told me of their pain at losing someone dear to them and how they cannot continue. Some have been close to suicide. Giving a message from Spirit to them is a huge responsibility and one that needs care and compassion coupled with common sense.

On other occasions I have passed many apologies to a recipient of a message. This has allowed some people to move on, while others have refused the apology. To those who refuse I politely say that as a medium it is my job to pass the message on and it is entirely their choice to accept it or not. I also explain that sometimes it is helpful to the one in Spirit to have that opportunity to express their regrets and to say sorry for their actions or behaviour.

I find the most difficult but also the most rewarding messages come from children in Spirit. As sad as the information may be, children bring a sense of joy with them.

They are so excited to be with their family and to communicate their feelings. Children come with such strong energy that at times I feel I can skip forever or run a marathon. They lift everyone who hears their words and especially when they tell their parents or siblings how much they are loved and cared for in the Spirit world. They take great delight in giving away secrets, by telling on their siblings or reminding their parents that they can see everything. I recall one girl telling her mother that her brother had sweets in his pocket. The poor brother was on a diet and his mother was trying to stop him eating too many sweets. That brought laughter to the mother and a frown from the brother.

When I first began to give Spirit messages, I was communicating a message to a young woman who worked in a school. Suddenly I was aware of a small boy. He then started to tell me that the young woman was having problems with two children in class. He told me their names. I passed this information to the young woman who was surprised but confirmed the names were correct and yes, both boys were causing her trouble during lessons. I then had to explain to the young woman that this small boy who was communicating with me had been a pupil at the school many years ago. He had been of poorly health and died before completing his school years. He also told me his full name and the name of his younger sister who had attended the school. He told the young woman not to fret over the boys as he would help to get them to behave. The young woman was concerned for the small boy as the school was being closed and would be derelict soon. She worried the small boy would be alone. I let her know that he only came around as he liked to see the children play. He would be alright and would find other ways to play. He told her that he was aware that she was not being treated kindly in the staff room by other teachers. Again, she confirmed this as true. She was delighted when he told her this would end when she moved to the new school. This young woman was really happy to receive this message but wondered why the small boy had been drawn to her. He told me it was because he liked her. It was my turn to be amazed when I later received information from the young woman to say she had checked school records and found the names of the small boy and his sister in a very old school register.

Children always bring a sense of happiness with them despite the sadness at their passing. Every time I find myself saying to a parent or sibling that their child, sister or brother just wants them to be happy.

It is imperative that each person is allowed to mourn the loss of a loved one. To be denied that opportunity is to build a barricade that prevents the expression of emotions. When emotions are supressed, the normal reaction to loss is hidden away. This can surely lead to internal anguish which in turn becomes prevalent in the physical. There is no time limit that is reached to suggest grief is over. No-one truly gets over grief but learns to live with it.

Many years ago I met a lady called Agnes, who became my Spiritual mentor and friend. She was a formidable lady who took no nonsense when it came to mediumship. Agnes was married to Joe, a lovely gentleman who always had a smile. She had a sister, Catherine. All three were often see together. All had a belief in the Spirit world. I had moved to live in Perth and had begun to seek help in developing my mediumship. I had always just believed I had a "knowing" which was unusual. As I sought answers I realised these "knowings" were in fact Spirit guidance and that I was a medium, whether I wanted to be or not. Eventually I found myself attending a Spirit Church where some elderly ladies were very kind to me. I was happy to make tea and just be in the background. My writing then was mostly poems or verses that would come to me. Some were quite religious which was not really my thing. These words were coming from Spirit although at the time I just thought it was my imagination. One evening at the Spirit church I was asked to read one of my verses. I was nervous standing on the podium. Being in front of an audience was a bit daunting for me even though I was used to speaking in public as a serving police officer. It was very different within a Spirit church.

On another Sunday evening the visiting medium had failed to show up. I was asked to go to the local hotel, use their payphone and phone a lady who was a medium and ask her if she could help out by doing the mediumship demonstration. That lady was Agnes. I remember her giving a message to someone, then looking at me. She pointed me out and said, "I have to talk to you". She proceeded to talk as if in a trance and continued to talk to me for the rest of the demonstration, much to my embarrassment. The only part I recall was when she said "Lady, you will stand on this platform". When the service was over, Agnes spoke to me and gave me her telephone number and offered to help me with my mediumship path. Thus started a journey that lasted for over twenty years until her death. We would disagree and fall out on occasions, but I always respected her. Agnes had served many Spirit churches in her lifetime but had retired from the circuit when I met her. She took me under her wing and guided well. The last ten months of Agnes's life were hard. Joe had died the year before and Agnes had been diagnosed with lung cancer. Her sister Catherine had died a few years earlier. Agnes was on her own and I cared for her for those last ten months. We had many profound conversations during that time. On the nights when I slept on her small couch, I would feel tears sting my eyes knowing she would need my help if she took a turn for the worse through the night. I got to know the nurses, her doctor and the Marie Curie ladies who all looked after her so well. I know I grieved for Agnes even though she was still alive. I grieved for the lady she was and who she had become. I watched her slowly waste away so much that I was afraid to lift her in case I caused her pain. She was just skin and bone. There was one occasion while sitting with her she asked about "My Man". She meant the Spirit Doctor who had been working with me in a healing capacity. Agnes never really believed me when I told her about him. However, on this occasion, she asked for his help. Later that night in conversation with my Spirit guides I requested the help for Agnes. What a surprise I got next day when I arrived early to find Agnes sitting up in bed with a smile on her face. As soon as I sat down, she said "Well, your man has helped me". This was quite a surprise for me. There was another surprise for me too, when Agnes turned to me and said "I know you have it now" (meaning I was a medium and communicating with Spirit).

The day came when I had to call an ambulance and get Agnes to hospital. While in the recovery room, the doctor took me aside and said "Agnes is close to the end now". I walked back into the room and took her hand. She looked at me and said, "I have to leave you now". She passed to Spirit a week later. Despite my knowledge of Spirit and my grief, I couldn't bring myself to cry. My job was to arrange the funeral and sort her property. I threw myself into ensuring all was done as she had wished. Suddenly a year had gone by, and I had still not shed tears. Then a few days before the first anniversary of her death I attended a demonstration of mediumship by the well know medium, Tony Stockwell. He gave me a message from Agnes and I felt the tears fall. The memories came flooding back and grief hit me hard. It took some time before I returned to my Spirit work. I can say the feelings that I experienced were beneficial to me and helped me to be more considerate of others, especially when delivering Spirit messages.

The need for balance in our lives is crucial to any existence. A balance of life ensures we can love, heal, rest and be grateful for all we have. It gives the time to work, to play, to just be. When grief enters our world that balance is disrupted.

Time has no meaning and finding a sense of peace is nigh impossible. Our sense of awareness is dulled and even the kindness of others seems not to be enough to lift us out of the despair and sadness. There are no easy solutions to recovering as each person mourns in their own way. A strong character does not necessarily mean a strong will to recover. A weak personality does not mean someone will fall completely to pieces. Finding the way forward is an unknown journey that throws up many challenges. It is not an easy journey but with self-compassion it can be travelled in a way that permits those who grieve to dictate the length of time needed to return to a happier state of mind. When the death is of a loved pet, it is the love of another pet that can bring some comfort. This can take a long time to manifest but the love shared with the lost pet is still within the owner. A new pet, received at the right moment, allows that love to be expressed again. Guilt is the emotion that can interfere with the ability to move on. We can feel that if we move on with life, we are forgetting our loved one. It is hard to judge the precise time when life begins to change to a more normal way of living. Family and friends, when trying to be helpful, can say or do something that causes distress or anger. Yet, it is family and friends who see the way grief is affecting us. It is they who notice the big and small changes in the behaviour of those who are grieving.

If I can offer any advice I would say to family and friends, please don't ignore someone who is grieving because you are frightened to say something which may cause the person to burst into tears. Bursting into tears may well be what is required and needed. Don't be frightened of mentioning the deceased's name or talking about them. Speak of the good memories and allow smiles to return to the faces of the mourners. I recite here a poem given to me by Spirit;

"*Death is a doorway we all walk through*
 there is nothing to fear or to harm you
 the love you left will still be strong
 their tears will dry as life carries on
 your memory will remain in subtle ways
 while they learn to live through dark days
 you shall grow in death's shining light
 all will be well as you give up the fight
 accepting the grace of a divine loving father
 knowing you are home where loved ones gather."

WALKING TO THE LIGHT

As a medium I know that life is eternal. I have received enough information and evidence from my Spirit guides and from those who communicated messages using me as their channel. I still feel for those who struggle with their thoughts and emotions when death has visited their life. Not everyone is prepared or wants to accept that life is eternal. It does sadden me as I know my own belief is a huge comfort to me and I would want that comfort for all who grieve, but I must allow others to choose what they believe.

Finding ways to face each day is a challenge, even without suffering a loss. Those who were very dependent on the person or animal who has died are doubly at a loss as grief is increased by the sense of inadequacy. They may well feel they do not have the "know how" or "courage" to go on living. Making any decision is hard and reaching out for help is something they are wary of doing, not because they can't but because they are fearful of how their life will be changed even further. This is a regret for many who communicate with me. They tell me that they are worried for their family, friend or colleague left behind, who do not seem to be coping with life without them.

There is no easy fix to get someone back into the rhythm of life. Each individual has different needs and beliefs. Taking the first step can be daunting and requires much courage and support from family friends and professionals.

Learning to pass Through Darkness to Light, can be assisted by looking at Death, not in fear as conventional religions dictate, but as nothing that is final but instead as the doorway that permits entry into eternal life. Many religions will criticise this thought or action as something of the devil's work. In fact, as a medium, my work is decried by many religious orders. How sad this is, especially when we think of that wonderful man known as Jesus, a truly great healer and medium. Even the Bible relates stories of his remarkable work among lepers and the sick. It tells of his materialisation when his disciples saw him days after his death. He spoke with his disciples – indeed, he said, "In my Father's house there are many mansions. If it were not so, I would have told you. I go there to prepare a place for you".

We have religious leaders who speak of Heaven and Hell. They preach the need for attending church and to fear the Lord. How terribly tragic this is. Whether you believe in a God, Buddha, Mohammed or any other deity, surely any loving Father of any religion would not bring harm to his people. My own belief is that there is a greater Universal power - whether I call it God or not, does not matter. What I do know is Death, like life, is to be celebrated. Understanding and accepting my word may be difficult for some but coming to a realisation that the body we have is only to allow us to function in this our physical world. It enables us to experience all manner of situations, conditions, good and bad. This, then, gives us opportunities to learn and progress in every deed, every act, every emotional behaviour and recovery, so that we may become a balanced and astute person, who knows that kindness and compassion are far better than hatred and violence. Grief is only one lesson, albeit a distressing and hurtful lesson; it has the capability to transform our life in a way that allows each person to change and to bring about the harmony that a contented life so dearly needs. Knowing that your loved one who has died is not only at peace but is living on, in another world, call it a different universe or simply the Spirit realms (whichever sits comfortably within your psyche) surely must bring an element of freedom from the chains of mourning that restrict and suffocate rational thinking and the ability to continue living, not just in harmony but with a joyful heart.

Speaking of the Light, my Spirit guides and friends take great pains to tell me of their world and how the physical body, when left behind after death, becomes clothed in light. The consciousness of each person that lives on is housed in an ethereal body of light. The mind of the deceased at first may well be confused as it looks upon the new surroundings. Yet they are not alone and are soon brought to the knowledge that their earthly body, with all the aches and pains, no longer exists. It can take a while for some people to understand the revelation that they have not been destroyed, or left to "push up daisies". Their death was not the end. While each one is concentrating on the newness of eternal life, the ones left to grieve are suffering with thoughts of sadness and broken hearts. Here then is the interaction between both worlds as the deceased wishes desperately to let their loved ones know they are alive and well in Spirit, while the grieving just want one more chance to be with them, to hold them one more time or to tell them how much they were loved.

I urge you as you have read this far to think on this information and to take some comfort in this knowledge. We all know that Love is a powerful emotion and heals many ailments, mental, emotional, physical and Spiritual. Many will have heard the saying "Love never dies". How true is this statement? People are now looking to question the dictating of religious beliefs. No longer is society accepting the dogmas that blight our thoughts and leave us fearing the transition called death. Some churches are beginning to open their minds to the existence of life in another realm, modifying their teachings of a God of wrath, a God who judges and punishes. They are bringing forth the need to Love one another and to care for those who are unable to care for themselves. They are teaching forgiveness and compassion. These are two emotional issues that are much needed when grief is threatening to suffocate all reason. Allowing ourselves the act of forgiveness for anything that we feel we should have done or said to the one who died, is a step to recovery. Being compassionate to oneself gives the freedom to smile once again, to remember with a glad heart the life of the deceased. In present times, the burial or cremation of a body is not now a time of sorrow but an act of love in expressing the feelings and the gratefulness of having their loved one share a part of life with them. Funeral attendees have stopped wearing black, the colour of mourning, and are now clothed in colour or displaying favourite things of the deceased. Many who know they are nearing their final breath are requesting that they are remembered with joy and not sadness.

There is no guidelines or rules when it comes to recovery from grief. Each loss is unique as is every human being. The effects of mourning are not set in stone and will be entirely different for all.

Once the passage of time was classed as the healer and still is a good comforter but when one is in the throes of early grief, time is the enemy. The weeks after a funeral can be lonely, when relatives and friends have returned to their daily lives and the one who is lost in grief finds the quietness of their home is no longer protective but a place of solitude and past memories that add to the hurt and tears.

Such is the destructive strength of morbidity.

Listening to words of wisdom from my Spirit guide, Chang-Li reminds me that after a death we cannot expect time or life to stand still. As hard as these following words from Chang-Li sound, they are so right and such a pleasant way to bring someone through grief and into a place where they can see the light and wonders of life.

"Take pleasure in watching the birds feed or splash in a bird bath. Get in your garden and feel your fingers in the soil. Yes, your fingers will get dirty but know you are connecting to a powerful source of universal energy. If you have no garden, then walk in nature where there are trees, look closely at their branches, their roots and their leaves. See the intricate and beautiful weaving of Mother Nature. Hug the tree if you want and feel the vibrational energy flow through you. Stand by the sea, a loch or river and watch the flow. Nothing is too much trouble as the water passes over, around or through the obstacles. Watch the shores or the banks and see the life of the creatures that take food and strength from the movement, giving them sustenance.

Let the seasons and weather astound you with their glorious colours and tremendous ability to leave you awestruck.

Look to the animal kingdom for lessons in behaviour and the cycle of life.

Lastly look in the mirror and really see YOU, the you that was created for this life, then look inward and feel the beat of your heart, the emotions of your senses and know the real you are a Soul that is perfect.

Let go of the fear, let go of the thoughts that strangle your ability to live and know without a shadow of doubt that life is eternal and there will come a day when you will be with your loved one once again."

Blessings to you all, Chang-Li

I am aware that not everyone can carry out all of these recommendations from Chang-Li and he also prompts me to mention those who do not have the ability, sight or hearing to carry out such actions; but here would be an opportunity to show compassion to another person, by helping them, taking them, if possible to a garden or forest walk, or beside running water or the sea, where all the wonders can be described. Where you can let them smell the flowers, feel the textures. Paint the picture for the blind.

Be their eyes, ears or voice and let them experience the universal wonders of our world. We must not forget the sky, especially at night when the stars are bright, the moon is shining and some planets are visible.

The passing of the days, weeks, months and years will never erase the memories and the love felt between you and your loved ones who live on in the etheric realms. Maybe the memory becomes dull and vague, but the love remains. When that light at the end of the tunnel begins to grow bigger and seems to be shining brighter, it signals a chance to ease out of the darkness, to look at life with new eyes and see that the world still exists. Time may have changed some things but moving forward begins to become easier. You may find yourself able to look at the photograph of him or her, maybe your pet, without bursting into tears. You can smile at the good times you had and start to realise that the time you were together was a gift not to be tarnished with sorrow. Stepping into the light of life again creates the opportunity to shape your life in a way that brings pleasure through new challenges and new friendships. When you are smiling, so too will your loved one as they see you have found the strength to carry on. This physical world of ours is taxing and can cause us to experience many difficulties as we journey through. Yet we must remember that it also provides wonderful moments of joy that uplifts and inspires us.

Many mediums will speak of the choices we have and that we must remember that we are a Soul in a physical body, here to learn. The pains we feel within and through this body are not permanent. When death visits, it frees us from the shackles of physicality. We become the Soul, clothed in light. The burdens of the physical body are removed. Our mind or consciousness continues to exist in Spirit. How we behave in this world will determine how we progress in Spirit.

That story you may have been told as you grew up about death and how you will be judged by God or maybe the devil for your deeds, good and bad, is a fallacy. Only you can judge your life and how you lived it. Whilst in Spirit, your sense of right and wrong is heightened and you will feel the hurt as you come to realise how your actions caused hurt to another. The same applies to the good and kind behaviour when you see the effect you had on someone who appreciated your conduct or actions.

Eternal life can be filled with contentment or resentment. The choice is yours, so why not start to develop your thoughts towards those of love and compassion. Forgive yourself indiscretions and try to be a better person. This, too, will bring smiles to your family, friends and pets in Spirit.

To walk back into the light of life is a challenge, but there are ways in which one can help oneself. There will come a time when the tears begin to subside or you no longer have tears left to cry and feel numb. This is a chance to think of your loved one and all the good times you shared. Look out old photographs, especially those that make you smile. Go through the years with the photographs and put them in order, from their young age, to school years, to teenage and adulthood or to the age they reached before passing to Spirit. Build up their story. Put them in a book that you can look at when you feel low.

Years ago, there was a television programme called "This Is Your Life". It was hosted by Eamon Andrews and later by Michael Aspel. They had a big red book with lots of photographs and memories, including experiences of the guest who was to be selected for the show. It took the guest back to times and people in their life who were part of their life's journey. The other guests were known to the selected participant and shared their memories, which brought much laughter and sometimes tears. It was a happy programme, with many stories being told of how life had brought the people together and what some people meant to others. When you are creating your book of photographs add stories from your memory that will help you feel better and keep your loved one's life ever present. This is one way to give you comfort and courage to step forward and start to live knowing you shared your life with someone special. It lets you see that you can continue to make memories and as you grow stronger, please believe that your loved one in Spirit will be so happy to see you go on living and finding joy again.

Memorials are another way to remember someone and show how much you loved them. It can be an occasion, not just for family but for friends and colleagues to come together and share their memories of the one who has died. It can be very enlightening when you hear stories about your loved one and how they interacted with others, through friendship or work. A memorial can be held soon after the funeral or maybe on the first anniversary of the passing.

Some people may be happy to visit the gravesite or memorial garden. In my work as a Medium I try to encourage close family or friends not to make this an everyday occurrence as it can become a ritual that will thwart the progress of grief and threaten the emotional health of those who are grieving. Knowing that our Soul or consciousness lives on after physical death brings the awareness that the body that lies in the grave is only that – a body that clothed your loved one whilst they existed in our world. The very real Soul that was your loved one has survived the transition we call death and is more alive than ever in the etheric realms or, if you like, in the Spirit world. When delivering messages from someone in the Spirit world to a relative here, I am saddened to hear them say their loved one is crying at the graveside every day or week. I know from my experiences with Spirit that this is not healthy and will not bring peace to the heart of the griever. It may appease them to know they have visited and paid their respects, laying flowers and keeping the grave site looking fresh and tidy, but many times the loved one in Spirit wishes the flowers to be enjoyed in a home or garden.

Taking the opportunity to bring the light back into our lives is a testament to the love felt for the deceased. Remember they loved us whilst with us and still do, even though they are not physically present.

There are some deaths that feel so unfair that it makes it harder to accept and to find a way out of the grief cycle. I share a story here that is truly sad. The loss of a son who was dearly loved. A son who found this world too hard to live in and had his struggles, then found a new outlook only to be struck down with further tragedy. Mhairi's son was only thirty two when he passed away after suffering from oral cancer. Mhairi herself has a firm belief in the Spirit world and the wonderful ability of communication between the two worlds.

MHAIRI'S STORY

"Niki was our oldest son. He had suffered severe mental health since he was a young boy. He was diagnosed with an early onset psychosis around seventeen. Specialists believed it to be schizophrenia but diagnosis at this age was difficult.

Niki struggled all his adult life with severe social anxiety, making any family get together extremely difficult for him and the family. In a way, we grieved for a son we struggled to reach. I knew he was there but fighting through the health issues was extremely hard. It was common for Niki to talk of suicide and we would spend our lives waiting for the next moment it would rear its ugly head.

Niki seemed to be in a better frame of mind when he was diagnosed with an aggressive mouth cancer. It had just looked like a bad mouth ulcer on his tongue. The whole family felt that this was a blow too far and that Niki had been dealt a tough hand already. He underwent very invasive surgery removing two thirds of his tongue and rebuilding it from wrist muscle and skin. The operation for Niki, albeit horrendous, was a piece of cake compared to the hospital stay and he struggled in the environment assuming staff were talking or laughing at him. He couldn't wait to get out and made quick progress, leaving early against the advice of the staff. He later had to undergo chemotherapy and radiotherapy that played a toll on his already frail body. Eventually they had to stop as the danger to his organs was too much of a risk. After being given the all-clear, he was looking forward to Christmas. His favourite time. Niki was such a giver and loved the joy on the faces of those receiving his well thought out gifts. It was a bittersweet time as when it was over his mood dipped badly and he was convinced the cancer would return. Sadly, it did and on his Godmother's birthday in February we received the news that it was terminal. My heart broke. All the fighting and the struggle to get him to stay in hospital and his anxiety on high alert for what? – nothing. We made the decision that he would spend his remaining time with us as there was no way he was going back to hospital. I remember the day we found out that it was terminal. I was sitting on my bed and saying to Niki,

"There is nothing to be afraid of, you will be letting go of a life that has been hard, for a better one. You have learned your lessons you were sent here to learn and now it is time to go home. You won't be alone, you have loads of family who love you and they will be there to meet you when the time comes".

I also told him,

"My friend Heather will make sure you are okay, as well as your Grandparents and a favourite Uncle".

Niki was frightened and asked if he would struggle to breathe and I said, "No. You will be given oxygen if you need it".

Little did I know; for nearly two months we cared for him, staying awake to stop him facing his fears alone. His brothers would come home and take him out to go skating, a passion they all shared when they were younger. After three or four weeks he no longer had the strength and he would sit in his room, occasionally coming down to play a tune or two with his Dad on the guitar. It was healing for Niki having him do something to help his Dad learn.

The hardest part was that Niki did not want anyone to know he was terminally ill. Apart from the four of us we hadn't shared this with anyone bar a few very close friends. Niki didn't want friends or family to know as he was scared of the onslaught of visitors. However, his days were numbered. We eventually told family just days before he passed. Sadly, he died the day his Godmother came to assist with his care. She had bravely arrived. He got his wish. We respected what he wanted.

I began to grieve for Niki long before he died. I feel like I have been grieving all of his lifetime. I grieved the first time he asked whether he would ever meet someone and have a family, knowing it would never happen. I grieved when he realised this.

We spent our lives waiting on a phone call to say he was found dead, only for cancer to take him when he finally decided he wanted to live. We surrounded him with love as he took his last breath; his Dad, Steve and I at his head cradling him and his brother Dean at the foot. His brother Ally couldn't bear to see Niki like this, so he waited downstairs.

I remember the stream of cousins popping in to say their goodbyes - his brothers and two cousins playing Niki's new game console and celebrating his life with a bottle of malt as Niki's shell of a body lay still whilst they tried to beat his score. We left them there until they were ready to let him go.

I don't think I will ever be ready to let him go. My heart breaks thinking of how difficult he found life and part of me is so happy he no longer needs to suffer. Yet the mother in me cries to hear his laugh and see his beautiful face. I remember the time he finally realised he was a beautiful person. Sadly, it had to wait until his body was emaciated and weakened by cancer. He thought thin meant beautiful, not the shine in his eyes, the love in his heart and the kind and caring soul that he was. How I miss this. I still make the mistake of calling my two other sons by his name. This is because I think of him as here. Sometimes I feel he is more here than he was when he was alive. I think him, feel him, visualise him. I talk to him, I continue to love him.

. . .

My grief was for the pain he endured through his life and the dying process, for the torture of his treatment being trapped in a situation that filled him with fear, with no escape. He did try. For what I can no longer see. I do not grieve for his new life. I am happy he can be who he truly is. I love when he comes through with a message like "Give Dad a break", because I truly know it is my Niki and I love him so much.

There was a time when I heard him call my name as I was alone at home and I questioned "Did I hear that?" The most beautiful moment for me was when Niki spoke through the medium Sandy Campbell when he was in the trance state. Niki called my name and what did I say - "What son?" It was the most natural thing for me to say. I know he's here. I spend less time in grief and more trying to be able to bring joy to others that have lost loved ones."

Mhairi K Forfar

We sometimes forget how we first reacted when our close relative, friend, colleague or pet died. The ensuing days, weeks, months and years play tricks with our memory. Then, as we realise, time has passed without our thoughts being intensely on the death, that brings guilt, as feelings of letting them slip from our mind is like a burden that makes us suffer even more. So many different emotions cloud our rational thinking when grief takes over. The ups and downs continue to occur and happen just as we think life is beginning to get easier and we are finding ways to get through the day without crying or wishing we too were with them in spirit.

. . .

The stories I have been privileged to share are wonderful and yet heart-breaking. The words written by those who were honest enough to say what loss and grief meant and did to them are inspiring and truly heart-warming.

No-one really knows how they will behave as they tread wearily through grief. While some can throw themselves into work or a project to help them move on, others see no way out or forward.

Death through a tragedy, disaster or suicide brings more questions than answers when grief penetrates. Those unanswered questions are a weight that never gets lighter. The "what ifs" and "why's" and "how could I not have seen it coming?" all remain constantly in the mind of those trying to fathom the loss and still go on living. When the death is expected through a terminal illness it may give time for creating precious memories and for preparing for the inevitable, but it doesn't in any way ease the pain that will come and affect the lives of those who remain. Some may feel that they had time to say and do all they needed to before they passed away. So too will those who cared for the dying, knowing that speaking and showing how they feel will bring some comfort after the passing.

Although this may be pertinent for many, there are some who are unable to accept the inevitable and cannot find a way to express themselves. Some may not wish to discuss plans to assist the dying person, or even to tell them they are dying. This is not selfish or ignorant. It is a coping mechanism and it gives a sense of hope, that all is not lost and giving up is not an option.

When a child dies, no matter the age, parents, grandparents and older relatives all feel that the natural order of life has been denied. To bury a child is beyond comprehension for most. It seems so unjust and unfair. Illness that causes the death of a child is hard and brings to the fore how vulnerable we all are. When a child is killed in an accident, those close will blame themselves or feel they failed to protect the child. The unlawful taking of any life, never mind that of a child, is devastating. The turmoil that invades the senses causes mental anguish to the point where medical intervention is required. The hurt becomes unbearable and the anger threatens the very essence of rationality. It is no wonder that lives are brought to a standstill and thoughts of revenge become, in some cases a reality.

Children are precious and it is my belief that none are born evil. It is the way of life and behaviour of others that can be the catalyst for someone becoming cruel and vindictive to the extent that they feel the need to destroy others.

Grief doesn't easily recognise forgiveness and the strength and depth of it can overwhelm the most compassionate person. Yet forgiveness will be a crucial part in recovering from a loss. It allows us to forgive ourselves as well as those whose actions turned our world upside down.

Forgiveness and compassion are tools that are useful in taking steps in the recovery process. Forgiving does not mean forgetting. Compassion does not mean weakness.

Looking toward the light of day when life will become more acceptable and less painful, is accomplishable when we realise that our loved one is surviving, albeit on a different wavelength or vibration. As a medium, this knowledge for me is what sustains me and allows me to work with Spirit. Knowing their words and messages bring a sense of peace and comfort to the recipient in such a way as to begin the healing process that will eventually lead to a more settled way of living.

Mediumship may not be everyone's cup of tea. Seeing the look of relief and the smile on someone's face, who moments earlier had the look of pain deeply etched on their brow, is something that cannot be dismissed. It is very rewarding for any medium.

I would like to share a story here from a man, a father to a young son, who lost his wife, his soulmate to cancer.

ANDREW'S STORY

"In 2010, Tania, my wife, was diagnosed with cancer. I remember that moment in time like it was printed out and stuck up on the wall. It was 16th November, and I had just returned home from dropping our son Gabriel at school, which was a short distance away from our home. On returning, I heard the phone ring. My wife was working from home and answered it. I could hear her talking. She said, "Doctor, if this is serious then tell me". She went into her Salon and closed the door.

Some six months prior, Tania had noticed a lump on her right side. She had gone through various tests and ended up seeing a urologist who diagnosed water cysts and advised her that it was nothing to worry about. This later proved to be a severe misdiagnosis. A further six months down the line Tania was experiencing terrible pain in her neck. She was sent for an MRI (magnetic resonance imaging) scan. The phone call on 16th November was the Doctor calling with the result. The Doctor told Tania that bone lesions had been found on her vertebrae. I could see how disturbed my wife was and we immediately turned to the internet to find out what this meant. The answer we found was that bone lesions are a secondary cancer condition. We attended the Doctors practice, and it was confirmed they were a secondary cancer and investigations would have to be done to find the primary cause of the cancer. We both shuffled out of the Doctor's surgery. It felt like we were in a fishbowl looking out at the world which was carrying on as normal with people doing their day to day business while time seemed to stand still for Tania and me. For ten days we were both in a state of shock, then we started to discuss our options including looking into alternative treatments. We also had to consider Gabriel who was only seven years old. We came to the decision not to tell him. We told a few people in the village where we lived. We didn't want too many people knowing just in case someone said something to him. The last thing we wanted was to cause him terrible emotional damage. This diagnosis altered our very existence and our plans for the future, became secondary to what was now happening. Nothing was making sense anymore. We felt we had an impending sentence hanging over us. The next months were filled with hospital visits for numerous tests which eventually found the primary cause of the cancer. It was her right kidney. A decision was taken to remove the right kidney.

After the operation, Tania seemed to regain her strength and her general health improved, which was very positive. More tests were conducted and it was decided that Tania should have chemotherapy. This would entail six sessions at three weekly intervals. These would take place over the festive period. We were told by the oncologist that after three sessions of chemotherapy they would check to see if she was responding well to the treatments and if she was, then the last three sessions would be completed. If she wasn't responding the oncologist would discuss with us what was likely to happen and how long Tania may survive.

    Watching my wife's health and overall spirit responding to the chemotherapy was in itself challenging. I would watch as she would spend several hours being sick for several days at a time. After the chemotherapy sessions were completed we had a meeting with the oncologist. I asked if it was appropriate to take Tania on a holiday. I saw Tania's face light up when I suggested we return to her home country of South Africa for a holiday. The holiday was booked for April 2012. Two weeks before we were due to go on holiday, I returned home and found Tania in the kitchen. She was staring out the window and tears were running down her face. I hugged her and asked, "What's wrong?" Tania said she couldn't live in this country (Scotland) anymore. I responded by saying we would return to South Africa for good if that was her soul's desire. At that, she cried more tears.

There were many strange thoughts and emotions going round in my head. Tania would struggle to sleep at night and my mind was racing. I was concerned that our move back to South Africa would compromise any treatment she may need. In South Africa the medical system is expensive, especially the treatment of cancers. We could not get medical insurance because of her existing condition. At these times I used my love of music to get me through. It was my go-to therapeutic practice. I composed a piece of music to reflect my emotions. To this day listening to it haunts my emotions. I named the music "Rebirth". This was not religious in any way but it reflected the impact this had on our lives. Everything had changed. Over and above was the consideration of Gabriel. International moves and changing schools would have an effect on him. We had lived in New Zealand for four years because the policies in South Africa meant white males were excluded from employment opportunities.

The process to move back to South Africa began. I would stay in Scotland to sort out our business interests and ensure all accounts were up to date and everything submitted to the tax departments. It was a trying time as we had to arrange transportation of furniture and a car. It was a huge administrative task. Tania and Gabriel went ahead and flew to South Africa. I was to follow when all was finalised in Scotland. I had concerns for Tania as to whether she would need more treatment. The relationship with her family was fraught. Her brother did not like me and he was very controlling of her, so I had arranged for Tania and Gabriel to stay with friends. One day I received a strange message on my social media site. It was from Gabriel saying, "Daddy, Mummy has fallen". I had spoken to her the evening before and she had seemed fine. I immediately telephoned her brother and was told she had collapsed while making breakfast. He seemed to be in a state of shock and said he would call me back. I eventually found out that Tania had taken a sleeping pill mistaking it for a painkiller. Gabriel had seen Tania collapse and it had frightened him. I then found out that Tania and Gabriel had been staying with her brother and sister-in-law. This was a mystery to me as I had arranged for them to stay in a rented cottage owned by our friends. I didn't raise my concerns as I didn't want to add any stress to Tania.

The time came for me to fly to South Africa and I was eventually re-united with Tania and Gabriel. I could tell he was glad to see me. It was a hugely emotional time. Tania was in bed and as she got up I could see how frail she had become. She was wobbly on her legs and had lost a lot of weight. She told me the hospice nurse had been visiting and administering morphine. I was so glad we were together again.

Over the next few months we faced many challenges. We were still remaining positive that Tania would be cured. We were exploring all the different avenues of medicine and treatments. We were eventually told by a Doctor that he believed there was not much hope for Tania and he refused to treat her any further. He told me to prepare for the worst. This was a real crazy time and we had no support structure in place to help. I was planning everything around Gabriel, getting him to and from school. There were many administrative tasks too. Tania had a fall and she had to be taken to Johannesburg general hospital. As we had no income this was the only way to get her care. Tania was in the hospital for ten days and underwent radiation treatment. After this treatment I had to get Tania into a hospice as she was so weak and unable to walk. Tania was in the hospice for a number of weeks. I was billed for an extensive amount of money. This caused me more and more stress. I managed to find a frail care centre called Abbey Cross Lodge. They had space and took Tania in. I found myself supplying items via a chemist as this hospice was poorly funded. The policy of the centre was similar to that of the hospice and that was just to administer morphine. At times it was difficult to have a conversation with Tania due to her induced morphine state. By this time, Gabriel was aware of his mother's condition and was beginning to struggle emotionally. A decision was made not to take him to visit anymore although he did speak to his Mum on the phone. During this very emotional time one of Tania's friends tried to help by discussing a conversation she had had with Tania in the centre. Her friend told me Tania had said she just wanted to die and couldn't take anymore. In my fragile emotional state I could not accept this and began to cry. This really hit me hard. It was evident that Tania was deteriorating but we had not given up hope. Tania's friend left and I cried for hours. I felt confused, alone and went through all sorts of emotions. I pulled myself together for the sake of Gabriel. I had to face the probability that one of the worst moments of our life was approaching.

I visited Tania in the centre and although she was sitting up in bed and staring at the television, I could see she was in a daze. I took her hand and she turned to me and said, "Andy I am waiting to die". I did not know what to do - her eyes were empty, and she had aged ten years since the previous day. She asked me to leave as she wanted to be alone. I kissed her and could see the tears rolling down her face. I went to my car, I was shell-shocked and in a daze. I was scared and felt I was having a panic attack. A wave of anxiety washed over me and my lungs felt like they were collapsing. I couldn't breathe, I was shaking and felt myself hyperventilating. I was crying. Just then my phone rang and I saw it was Gabriel. I pulled myself together and answered. He was asking if I was ok and telling me he loved me.

Sometimes the normality of life is helpful so we had a Bar-B-Que and Gabriel and his friend were laughing and happy. I would even have a swim in the pool. Anything to give my mind a break. Then on the 11th January 2013, Tania's brother called and told me that Tania had passed away. I was shocked and my reaction told Gabriel his mum had died. He burst into tears. We were both shaking and crying. The shock of being told clouded my judgement. I couldn't send him to school. I took him to an amusement arcade. I guess I was trying to take his mind of his Mum. I couldn't think straight. I remember talking to a friend of Tania's on the phone. I can't remember what we did the rest of that day. The shock affected me to the point I was lost. Then I got to thinking why had Tania's brother been notified and not me, her husband? Her brother had been with her in her final moments, not me. It really should have been me. That hurt.

Gabriel and I had been attending loss counselling leading up to her death and I knew it was better to continue, especially for him. The counselling definitely helped. I felt relieved that Tania had passed as she had been in a lot of pain and discomfort. She was merely existing between morphine injections. Now that it had happened I knew I had big decisions to make for both Gabriel and myself. I knew we would move back to Scotland.

. . .

Tania and I had been married for seventeen years and the memories of all the trials we had been through were fresh in my mind. Now things were different - I was on my own now with Gabriel who was now nine years old. We had both gone through the most traumatic time of our lives and yet we have our treasured memories to help take us forward.

Tania and I had, on one or two occasions, spoken about the possibility of her dying but we had to keep going for Gabriel. The last few months of her life it became evident she was dying. When we were back in South Africa her family's behaviour, especially her brother's, was not helpful. He was quite controlling of Tania. After her passing her family cut us off which I felt was cruel especially for Gabriel. There didn't seem to be time to grieve and I wouldn't say I was in denial because we tried so hard to be positive.

The light at the end of the tunnel is still far off as I feel it is not just about losing Tania but also that Gabriel lost his mother. That has left a huge void and I know he is emotionally fragile. The journey is ongoing for me. My belief in the afterlife has certainly been a help. I have attended a few Spiritual groups and received a powerful message from Tania through a medium who knew nothing about me. The evidence given could not possibly have been guessed.

At times I think maybe we should not have moved back to South Africa. The medical services were not good and it was a drain on our finances.

. . .

The one thing that got me through and still does is my music. Writing music is a huge part of my therapy along with my creative art. Meditation helps me understand my place in the universe, allowing me to think more on my journey and the lessons I have learned and will continue to learn. If I had to give anyone advice, especially if they are going through a similar situation, I would say take care of yourself and think about the space you will be in if you lose your loved one. I made a lot of decisions on the spot and looking back, some were not the right thing to do. It took three years from diagnosis to her death. Such a tragic loss of my beloved wife took me from being a self-employed business consultant to someone who would lose their thoughts halfway through a sentence. I am so proud of Tania and of Gabriel. I am thankful for our life together and for having Gabriel. He is a lifeline for me."

Andrew Campbell Smith Scotland

The next story is from John. His journey to mediumship began after his father's death. John and his wife are both wonderful ambassadors for Spirit, serving Spirit centres and churches around the UK and abroad.

JOHN F'S STORY

"My father's terminal illness pre-empted my journey toward mediumship as I found myself in anticipatory grief. I had been attending development classes for several months and whilst I understood his Spirit would continue, I harboured a lot of pain at the thought of him no longer being physically with me. My father was a fighter, and it was testament to his character and his love for his family how he bore his condition with determination. Given the extent of the cancer in his body he was given two weeks to live. He endured for eighteen months, pushing through all pain barriers to be there for my mother and us. I visited my parents every day. In the weeks leading up to his death I noticed my father's frame diminish. We never spoke of my beliefs as my father was a devout catholic. On a particular evening in early December, he was staring beyond me. I knew he was looking at someone or something that wasn't me. I asked him,

"What are you looking at?"

He didn't respond and I then asked,

"Do you see someone Dad?"

He nodded his head and with tears in his eyes he replied, "Yes". He was so frail. I asked him,

"How many are there?"

He replied, "I don't know".

I asked, "Are there three?"

He smiled. All of his family were in the Spirit world, his parents and his only brother. I felt they were drawing near to help him. I knew it would not be long before he made his transition. My father battled bravely over Christmas and into the New Year. My birthday was 2nd January and he fought beyond that date, determined to ensure Christmas and my birthday would be joyous occasions. My father was extremely selfless. I was in awe of him. My heart was breaking. Two day after my birthday his fight was fading. My wife and I informed my siblings in the United Kingdom,and we prepared to be with him for his final days. He fought bravely.

. . .

Some seven years previously, my father had taken his first massive heart attack and whilst he was recuperating, we purchased a little transistor radio so he could listen to sport and the news whilst in hospital. He loved that little radio and it gave him some time out when he listened to it on old headphones.

When his health deteriorated and we were forced to place him into full time palliative care, we brought the radio up but never considered that he might listen to it. I think we just wanted to feel we were doing what we did before, in order to aide his recuperation. Deep down we didn't want to face the fact that he was dying. In his final hours as his body shut down, organ by organ, I sat holding his hand while my wife held his other hand. My mother was in the bed beside him in the care home. We were doing our best to comfort and support him and her. They had been married for sixty years and were devoted to each other. I sat with my back to the window and my heart was breaking. My strong father was physically wasted beside me. I let go his hand momentarily as mine had become stiff from stretching over the bedside. In my mind I sent out a thought to him. I was saying, "Dad if you can hear me, let me know, give me a sign that you know we are here, that this has not all been for nothing, that you know I am with you". I then noticed the transistor radio, and in my efforts to distract myself I picked it up, unwound the cables to place the headphones on my head. My wife remarked "the batteries must be flat on that". I tuned it on and loudly and clearly, I heard the song by Van Morrison, "Have I told you lately that I love you". This was the song at our wedding, when my Father and Mother danced beside us. The tears streamed down my face as I got my answer to the thoughts I had sent out. In my mind I said to Dad, "I love you too". I turned to look at him and take his hand again. He took his last breath and made his transition.

Over the years when I have struggled or had a particularly bad day, I have heard this song and always when I least expect it.

It comes on as I turn on the car radio or in a supermarket or whenever I have been in difficulty. For me it is our silent communication, a way to remind me that he is always with me, that when the chips are down, he supports me. For that I am eternally grateful. This understanding has helped me in the work that I do, and also enabled me to speak from a place of knowing. My Dad and my Mum are always supporting. What could be better than that?"

John Fitzgerald Ireland

I know it is strange to say that I find people who have a belief in the afterlife seem to be able to cope a little better with loss. The belief that one day they will all be together again helps to sustain them and gives the comfort and strength to move on with life. Even with the loss of a dearly loved pet, grief is felt just as hard. It can take some time before an owner has the feeling that they are ready to love another pet. The guilt can be debilitating as they think that their beloved pet will feel forgotten. I try to say to such an owner that their pet would be delighted that another animal is receiving the love and care they once did.

It is not everyone's belief. I must respect that, but if I can sow the seed that encourages someone to look beyond their own ideas of death and see the truth that life goes on, then I feel my work with Spirit is worthwhile. I must acknowledge also that there are some diehard sceptics that will never believe, even if a loved one was manifested in front of them. They will always find an answer or reason to disbelieve or to decry the possibility that communication with the Spirit world is possible. My own thoughts on sceptics are that they are essential to the work of Spirit in that they help ensure those who claim to be mediums or psychics purely for the wrong reasons are weeded out, and those grieving people are not duped or fleeced of enormous amounts of money. Sadly, it is a fact that there are some such characters in the Spiritual communities but then there are similar types in all walks of life. In a world that is filled with so many people of all descriptions, creeds, religions and genders, it is not difficult to see where beliefs are never straightforward and sometimes are undeniably disagreeable. What may seem to one group, a simple way of belief may indeed feel totally wrong for another group. That is why I need to consider my thoughts on life after death and not allow them to cloud my judgement when sitting opposite someone who firmly believes that "when you are dead you are dead". There is no changing such a person's mind and I would not even try to, yet I too am entitled to my beliefs.

When a time comes that brings death to anyone's door, life is touched deeply by the loss. The barrage of emotions that surface only add to the uncertainty of how one can deal with the aftermath. The circumstances of the death may prevent the family from the ability to say goodbye or even to view the body of the deceased. How hard that is to accept and to overcome the feelings of inadequacy or despair, knowing their loved one may well have been alone or in pain as they took their final breath. We are human and as such have human needs and to be unable to comfort or speak our true feelings to someone who is approaching their final journey can leave us devastated to the point where life holds no hope.

Solutions to working through grief are not always suitable for everyone. We are all unique and our coping mechanisms differ greatly.

One method that may be suggested is to look at ways of not falling into the rut of hiding our feelings of sadness and hurt. Many will be more comfortable keeping their feelings and thoughts within themselves, while others are likely to talk openly and freely to anyone who will listen.

At times when life seems to be moving on, we experience a memory stimulus such as a favourite song being played on the radio or finding ourselves visiting a place that was special to the deceased. This acts as a trigger for recalling the memories and the death. Here then is an opportunity to talk and release any hurt or anger that may have remained hidden deep within the psyche.

Another occasion that will prompt a return to the thoughts of the deceased is the anniversary of the passing, or their birthday. These times can bring about a recurrence of health issues especially for our mental health where our mind seems intent in creating the negative memories rather than allowing us to remember the good and happy times that were shared. Physical illness can become evident at these times. Stress can play a part in the weeks or days leading up to the anniversary or the birthday.

So how do we get to a point where we see the light? The light that shines brighter when we are more content in our ability to live, and to enjoy life without our loved one or our beloved pet. I am afraid there is no easy answer. The recovery period is not set in stone and may last until we are reunited through our own death and the transition to Spirit. Then as we rejoice in the welcome and presence of our loved ones gone before, we finally find peace. This next story has taken the lady many years to accept. The death of her husband by suicide had a great impact on her life. She found comfort in alcohol and with a tremendous effort found a way back to reality and began to live again.

ANNE'S STORY

"My husband Jim was abroad in his duty as an American sailor. He was in the port of Naples. On the 11th September 1993, he chose to end his life by hanging himself. We had been married for seven years and had two children aged five and three. I had returned to live in Scotland after three years in America.

I had been very homesick.

I had no idea that Jim had attempted suicide before. I knew he was unhappy. We had a heated telephone conversation and afterwards he decided to take his own life. I was working when I got the call to go home immediately. When I got home, two navy officers delivered the bad news and then left. I was in total shock at first, then real anger and fury took over. I was left with two children and no explanation. He left an apology letter to his fellow sailors but not to me and the children. What do you tell two children under six years of age?

Still angry, I immediately began to remove every photograph I had of him except the ones with the children. I wanted no memory of him in my life. It was so bad I threw myself into another marriage just eight months after Jim died. That marriage was a disaster from the start. I was so broken. I had to see a counsellor for one to one sessions. I was on anti-depressants. I spent five years like that and finally woke up one day, when I managed to stop taking the medication and get out of the dark place I was in. That's when the guilt and grief arrived. The guilt comes from not noticing your partner had an illness, not offering more compassion at the time and not being their rock when they needed you to be. The grief arrived because I had never really grieved and never went to his funeral. Normality came back to me around 2005. This is when I began to like myself again and stopped going on a journey of self-destruction with alcohol.

I can look at photographs of Jim now. I still feel sad when I think of him. Jim's death affected me a lot more than any other loss in my life. My outlook on life now is to never worry about things you have no control over and trust the universe to guide you. My outlook on death now is that it's part of living. Grieving is part of loving someone, knowing you will never see them again until it is your time to pass."

A Thomas Scotland

As can be seen in Anne's story the death of a loved one and the way in which they died can have a disastrous effect on how we behave and how we recover sufficiently to go on living. Suicide is never going to be an easy death to accept. However, there are times when suicide seems the only option for someone who is living with tremendous pain or a debilitating condition that will only progress and cause more devastating conditions of the body. The person affected knows what lies in store and cannot face the future. Suicide is their way of finding release from such horrible situations. They often feel it will be better for those who would have to watch their decline. They just want to end their pain and to allow their loved ones the freedom from the distress of seeing the deep suffering they are enduring.

. . .

Here is a story that confirms how much the deceased was suffering and how he could take no more. James was a dear friend of a fellow medium, Sandy, whom I know well. I saw and heard how James' death affected my friend. It still does. Here he tells of his friendship and his friend's death by suicide.

SANDY'S STORY

"James was one of my best friends. He shared the early days of my development with my mediumship. James and I attended the same two circles. I had met James before I even knew about my Spiritual ability. He was my cousin's partner. We became friends whilst I lived in Dundee with my sister. I was studying Musical Theatre in Glasgow. I would travel daily and at weekends and James would come to my sister's and we would spend time getting to know each other. It was great having someone to share the weekends, going to museums or just walking. We would sit and talk. I eventually had to move to London to complete my course. I was away for a year and on my return I found out from my cousin that he and James had parted company. He encouraged me to offer support to James as he didn't really know anyone in Dundee. I called to see James and this was the start of a great friendship. I had to complete a project for my degree and James helped me to organise an Arts festival as part of the process. On completing my studies I returned to live in Dundee. I set up a small community theatre company. James came on board and instead of being on the technical side he shared the stage. He was demanding and could be a drama queen. James was so lovable and everyone took to him.

. . .

One day, James decided to tell me more about himself and his family. He shared with me that as a young man he was diagnosed with Huntington's chorea. He took his time to explain what that meant. As his friend I listened and tried my best to be there for him. There were ups and downs with his emotions and his feelings.

In 2007 I went to see a local Dundee medium called Margaret. She gave me a reading and I was told I could do work for Spirit and that I was a healer medium and could also conduct a method known as Transfiguration and Trance (Transfiguration is where the medium's face appears to take the form of a Spirit communicator and Trance is where the medium is in an altered state and Spirit may speak through them). I was advised to find a Spiritual development circle. James and I had been attending the local Spiritualist Church in our area. We eventually joined their development circle. James had told me of some spiritual experiences he had experienced when he was younger. As time passed, the symptoms of Huntington's started to show. James' journey was not easy. There were times when he was not being given the chance to work with his mediumship but we got that sorted out. With the increase of Huntington symptoms so too did the involuntary movements increase and affected James and this would make him sweat as he tried to hide them. James still attended the development circle improving his healing and mediumship. He was so supportive of me. James and I would discuss life and death. James had looked after his Mum for many years. She had the same disease, so James was well aware of what was ahead for him. In 2008 James' Mum died. She quickly made her presence felt within our development circle. James found strength in being able to have that spiritual connection with his Mum. James and I had many talks about life and its meaning. It was great having James to share our Spiritual unfoldment and we would sit together to develop the altered state of Trance and share the wisdom of Spirit. Although James was a gentle soul he was a strong willed one. He could still smile through adversity. He would stand up for me when he felt I was being treated unfairly. James stepped back from spiritualism when he saw the negative experience I was suffering.

He didn't want to be part of something that was not of Love.

After his Mum died he opened up more to me about his condition and his plans. He even said that he had researched into travelling abroad and having a final holiday and then having his life terminated. This was hard for me to listen to and I found it heart-breaking, even though I knew life was eternal. James had always said he would not live to see the age of thirty-four. He taught me that life was for living and that we each had our own path and destiny. I encouraged James to find love despite his condition. I was so glad when he did. Although I never met his new partner, James would tell me about him. I recall giving James a message through Spirit that his partner would propose marriage to him. James didn't believe me. On a night when he was having dinner with his partner, he did propose with candles and all the trimmings, even getting down on one knee to ask James to marry him. However, for reasons unknown James turned him down. Sadly, the partner took his own life. James did get to see him in hospital and to say goodbye before he died. At a Spirit church in Edinburgh a psychic artist re-united James with his partner through a portrait she drew.

It was in 2012 when James was diagnosed with cancer. James had gone to hospital on his own as I was attending at a medium's house to receive a reading. James texted me with the news. James retreated into himself. He had done this on occasions before so we had agreed that if we did not hear from him by a certain time, we would notify the police. James attended his chemotherapy sessions alone despite me offering to go with him. He faced that journey bravely. He made it through the treatment for cancer and allowed me and his friends back into his life.

Christmas 2012 was our last together. I had sensed in the depth of my soul that he would not be with us by the following Christmas.

On the 22nd May 2013, James decided it was his time to depart this earth. He had often spoken of ending his life and said he would tell no-one. On that date I was attending a Spirit service in Dundee. I had asked James to come with me, but he refused saying he was busy. My last words to him were "I will see you through the week". My phone was switched off during the service. When the service was over and I switched it back on I received a voicemail with a message from James saying how sorry he was and he couldn't live anymore, he was ending his life. He was crying. I called my Dad and we rushed to James' house. It was too late. I knew that as his Mother and Gran had made themselves known to me from Spirit. They told me James was with them. My best friend, my brother, had transitioned to the spirit world. I was broken. I chose to continue working with Spirit as it brought me comfort.

Since James' death I have received many messages about him. People think because we are mediums we handle grief differently, but we have the same emotions and go through the same turmoil as everyone else. I miss him so much. James truly supported me on my spiritual journey and I have honoured him by naming a room in the Dundee Love and Light Spiritual and Well-being Centre. Sometimes it is who we meet that helps us grow and here was a stranger who became one of the most important people in my life. James encouraged me to write the words of Spirit. I share a poem I wrote after his passing."

GONE BUT NOT FORGOTTEN

You are always in my heart
Gone but not forgotten
The memories shall last
With each tear that I have shed
A smile will come shining through
Just as I remember
The love I had for you
Although you had to leave us
You left us with such grace
Upon the wings of an Angel
Where you could take your place
You stand now with the Angels
And Spirits up above
You are back gently in their arms
And you are smothered with their love
I know you will be watching
Over everything we do
We haven't really lost you
As in our hearts is a special place for you
So, fly free now you have your wings
You have no more suffering and no more pain
And learn and grow on the other side
Knowing we will be re-united once again.

A Campbell Dundee

Most mediums are happy to discuss their work with Spirit and how their bond with guides or helpers from Spirit help them as they journey through life with all its ups and downs. However, it does not make them immune to the grief and hurt when they lose someone they love. Personally, I know my belief that life is eternal and I will be with my loved ones again when I make my transition, is a huge comfort to me. This is why I try to communicate the messages from Spirit as compassionately as I can and, if asked, I will explain that my acceptance of life after death does not interfere with my religious beliefs.

For me it is more comforting to believe that life goes on after physical death than to think my loved one has rotted in a coffin or has been destroyed by cremation.

You may ask, "What of the grief caused by a different loss, such as a person's loss of physicality?" This next story tells of the loss of the husband a wife knew before a stroke robbed him of his physical and communicative abilities. He was an active serving policeman for twenty-eight years. Their lives changed forever.

SUSAN'S STORY

"Alan and I married when we were young. I was only eighteen. We had met while I was living and working in London. He was a cheeky lad and I remember our first meeting. He had brought my friends home from a night out and when he came into our flat. I stood up and he immediately took my seat, then he indicated for me to sit on his lap. He kissed me and I told him how forward he was and he should not be kissing me after just meeting me. I can still see this now after all these years. Alan did tell me he liked me because I was old-fashioned in my ideals. We have been married now for fifty-nine years. We married in the summer of 1969. He always calls me Sue, never Susan. We had a good marriage. A few years later along came our son. It was then I developed my condition - Rheumatoid Arthritis. It brought difficulties for me, but I kept positive. Alan had his career as a policeman and I eventually studied and qualified as a social worker, which was work I really enjoyed.

I loved Alan's character, he was cheeky, energetic, had a great sense of humour. He was helpful and caring but he did have a mischievous side and loved to play pranks. His eyes shone with devilment. He was a gentleman and looked after our wee family. I think he wasn't too keen on me working as he was a bit old fashioned too. He would have been happy for me to stay home and be a wife and mother, while he worked and was the provider.

Alan loved outdoors and we enjoyed many holidays together and as a family. In his spare time Alan would go walking and climbing the Munroes (hills over a certain height).

We used to visit my sister on a Sunday afternoon. I recall that on one occasion when we visited my sister she seemed more enthusiastic than usual. She told me she had got a new book on palm reading and was desperate to try out what she had learned. I was eager to oblige but Alan wasn't as he was sceptical about such things. Alan and I were in our forties, I was forty-five and Alan was forty-nine. I remember it clearly.

Initially we had a good giggle as she studied my hand and predicted my future. Then she said she saw a split from Alan when I was forty-eight. She studied Alan's hand and saw the same pattern on his palm. We didn't take it too seriously and pretty much put it to the back of our minds.

Then in 2000, just after I had turned forty-eight and Alan was fifty-one, he came home from work complaining of suffering from a migraine headache. I felt he had been overexerting himself in the gym and had caused the headache. Despite his headache he went to an art class but came home early. We decided to have an early night to see if it helped but around 2am. I was awakened by Alan pulling at my leg, in an effort to wake me up. I sensed something was far wrong and jumped out of bed, putting the light on. I saw that Alan was in obvious distress. I sensed he was having a stroke and telephoned for an ambulance. I called my son and a neighbour whom I knew was a retired nurse. They were a help to me until the ambulance arrived.

Our life of thirty years, as we had known it, really ended that night. Alan was in hospital for seven months before returning home a much different man. This stroke had caused full right-side paralysis, loss of memory and speech. Prior to this and the earlier accident (Alan had suffered serious injury after a fall while climbing) he had been a very active man. He had served as a Police Officer for twenty-eight years. He had been such an energetic outdoors man who loved bagging Munroes. He had done lots of dangerous pursuits, canoeing the Caledonian Canal, abseiling down a tall building and walking the West Highland Way; all to raise funds for arthritis research and other charities.

He was a family man who took great pleasure in spoiling me and our son.

I will never be able to erase from my mind his harrowing loud wailing followed by hard sobbing when I entered the hospital ward just as the Doctor was informing him all that he had lost physically and that it was permanent. He knew his career in the police service was over and that he could no longer climb mountains. His distressing response to this news has stayed with me, even after all these years.

I was glad my husband had not died that night, but I felt overwhelmed with the responsibility of managing his care. I had chronic arthritis which had caused severe restrictions to my own abilities. I worried about how I could keep his mood positive and find alternative ways for him to enjoy life. I could see he felt he had let his family down and that there would not be much going on in our lives after this. We cried together many times in the first few months after he returned home. I missed the Alan I knew terribly. We would be sitting next to each other, and the tears were rolling down my face. He seemed to understand my pain and together we grieved for his previous life and our lifestyle together.

After a period of time my mood improved and this enabled me to start fighting back and be grateful for what Alan could still do and for his amazing fighting spirit. We pulled together and started to plan trips away. Initially we went with friends, or our son, for support and to build our confidence in holidaying again. A saving grace for us was the Police Convalescence and Rehabilitation Centre in Auchterarder, Perthshire. It provided the physical and emotional rehabilitation which motivated Alan to get back to his painting. He began to paint with water colours while he listened to classical music. It was very healing for his soul and for mine to see him content.

Over a number of years, we spent many weekly breaks at the centre. However, Alan's condition deteriorated to the point he was unable to attend. We both miss going there. We miss the longer holidays we had, both abroad and in Scotland. Alan developed bowel cancer and his health declined even more. I was unable to take him away from home.

When I retired from my position as a social worker we moved to the coast. We have met many special people in the community and at church, who have shown us such kindness. It has been a good move for us.

Looking back, I remember feeling unimaginable grief when my father died in 1983 and I have known grief from the death of other family members, but I was not prepared for feeling so much emotional pain in seeing my husband come to terms with the physical and mental deficits caused by the stroke.

At the time it was hard to share what I was feeling with my son and other family members. My son is deep and he won't talk about his father's condition. He has always poured his heart out in birthday and Christmas cards and continues to do so.

My sister's prediction from the palm reading had come true as, in a way, there was an ending to Alan and my relationship as it had been. I felt I had lost my husband and at times gained a child. However, we began a new, and as it turned out, a richer and stronger relationship, which will stand us in good stead whatever the future holds for us. I find myself preparing for the possibility in the future of a life without Alan. I have anticipated the pain and possible loneliness when I no longer have my caring role; therefore, to help me adapt to a new future, I joined a philosophy and writing group. I represent carers on our local joint integrated Health and Social Work Partnership Board and I am an active member of the Seniors Action Group. I have forged firm friendships within these groups and with fellow church members and neighbours.

I have got used to the way Alan is now. I suspect or imagine I may feel some sense of relief for both of us if Alan should pass away. I won't know who to grieve for - I will have to fathom it out. Do I grieve for the Alan before the stroke or the Alan after it? I will make the time to grieve which hasn't been possible as my time has been consumed over the past twenty years juggling work and meeting Alan's needs.

Our life was going along nicely but the carpet was taken from under us when he had the stroke. Our relationship was equal before, but I am more of a carer now.

My advice to anyone is to live in the moment, appreciate what you have as things can change in an instant.
Alan is still with me now and life goes on."

Mrs Susan Dodd Ayr

Another story is from a friend. Her husband died before her eyes. Her story re-iterates how death and life are intertwined. How life changes in an instant.

<u>A FRIEND'S STORY</u>

"It was Easter 1987. My husband and I had been away for the weekend to Wales. When we arrived home, we took our clothes upstairs. My husband sat on the bed, made a groan, and fell onto the floor. I rang the Doctor who came and pronounced him dead. I had trouble taking this in and although I knew he had gone, my mind had trouble accepting it.

The day after my husband's funeral, my Dad collapsed. He died six weeks later. My Dad was an active man. If he had survived, his leg would have been amputated and he would never have coped with that. In a way his passing was a relief. I feel Dad was glad to go. Many times, I would think of my husband, and Dad was always there in my mind too.

It was hard to deal with the death of my husband and Dad.

Bereavement hits you and everyone deals with it in different ways. I dealt with it by working full time and this helped me enormously. I worked in a very busy office and the people around me were so considerate and helpful. They did not fuss over me but let me know they were there if I needed them. I keep in touch with them to this day. In relation to getting over the deaths, I don't think I ever really have. I have learned to cope and taken up challenges, leading to the different path I now lead.

I was never concerned with Spiritual matters and didn't really believe in life after death. After the night my husband died, I started thinking that someone cannot be there one moment and gone the next. I believe we are electricity and water and something has to be left. Nothing can be destroyed – just a change in vibration. One night after the deaths I was just lying in bed and could smell a horrible scent – like the smell of decay. At the place where my husband died I saw a mist rising. I had no idea what it was but have since found out it is a substance called ectoplasm. I found this out as I began to enquire at a Spiritual Church in Tunbridge Wells. I was not looking for messages from Spirit. I really wanted to know if my husband and Dad were alright. Were they safe and happy wherever they were?

I was a little disillusioned by some of the talk as all the people seemed to want was to be Spiritual. I did meet some very nice people and made some good friends. I did receive a message from a medium to say that I would be able to touch and feel my husband again. I replied to that medium that was not possible as I had burnt (cremated) my husband. It caused a stir in the Spirit Church. However, I did feel drawn to study to become a Spiritual Healer, with the members of the Spirit Church helping me. I even went onto become a bereavement counsellor and am now qualified to teach students to become bereavement counsellors. My life changed dramatically after the deaths of my husband and Dad."

Anonymous, Scotland

Even a belief in life after death does not make grieving any easier. It helps to know our loved ones will be cared for and will continue to thrive in their eternal home, but it never dulls the pain of loss.

This next story is from a lady who has had to cope with the deaths of her mother, father, brother and a close friend.

MICHELE'S STORY

"My Mum died in 1990, three years after I got married. I would often smell the fragrance of Lily of the Valley flowers which, for me, was an indication that Mum was close by. My Mum knew I wanted these flowers in my bouquet at my wedding, but unfortunately they were out of season. I missed Mum and her unconditional love. To smell this scent was comforting for me.

My Dad died in 2014. He had been in hospital since December 2013 until his passing on 3rd February 2014. I felt I had begun to grief before he died. My brother Michael and I had visited daily but this did not stop me from feeling helpless as I watched him deteriorate. I still think I was in denial as I kept thinking he would get better and come home. I watched as he became unable to eat or drink, refusing to be fed intravenously. I had taken the night of his passing off. The guilt I felt at not being present with him as he passed tortured me for a long time. The blame I put on myself for not being there to hold his hand was eating away at me. I would become angry at myself, feeling I should have known he was nearing death and should have made the right decision to be with him that night.

Shortly after Dad died I had a vivid dream. In it, my Dad came to me. He turned and looked closely at me. The dream was so real, I felt he was actually with me and was letting me know he was ok. This was a comfort to me. It took about one year to come to terms with Dad's death, although I miss him to this day.

My brother Michael died in 2018. He was my older brother, my rock and my guidance. I was his little sister. He always looked out for me, gave me strength and would make things right. His death left a huge void in my life and had a detrimental effect on my health (I now suffer from a Hiatus Hernia). Maybe it's a coincidence but that's a hole that needs filling, just like the hole left in my life without Michael. Michael had been in hospital for a short time. He was bleeding internally but we felt he was on the mend. He came home. A short time later he suffered a heart attack and was taken from this world. His death shook my world and turned it upside down. I miss him so much. His absence in my life still causes me pain. Once again, a dream brought Michael back to me for a moment. In the dream he stood facing me. He told me, "left hand side and heart". I took this to mean he had suffered an aneurism, burst blood vessel which caused his death.

Since my Dad's and Michael's passing, my belief in an afterlife has grown stronger and my curiosity of life in Spirit has deepened. I have attended courses to gain knowledge of how it all works. I have also visited mediums and been given evidence that my family are still existing and living in an etheric world, where we all return to when this physical life ends. Messages I have received through Spirit mediums, including Eleanor, have brought me love, guidance, hope and have helped to guide me through my grief. To know my family are well and free of pain is a great comfort to me.

The most recent death that has affected me has been the passing of my friend Trudy. She died in 2018. Trudy was my life-long friend. We had known each other since we were ten years old. She was there for me through thick and thin. She certainly was a good friend to me in my moments of grief. I had dreamt of Trudy the week before she passed. It was strange in that Trudy spoke to me, saying "It's time, Shell" (Trudy always called me Shell, never Michele). I knew this dream was letting me know that she and I would not speak again as she would die soon. Trudy had withdrawn from life. She would not answer my calls or texts. She did not want visitors. Although I understood, I found it hard not to keep contact as I so wanted to help ease her pain. The dream became special to me as it was a way of preparing me for her death.

I miss all my family and Trudy and still feel the pain of their loss. In my grief I sought help from my Doctor who recommended counselling. I have found that the messages I receive through Spirit mediums has been my greatest help and support and has given me a new outlook. I realise that life can be taken away at any moment and I am responsible for my own life and how I live it. Though I still grieve, I do so in the knowledge that life is eternal and we will meet again."

Michele Taylor High Wycombe

As you can see by Michele's story, grief has a way of causing us to change our outlook and even encourages us to seek more knowledge about death and life beyond. It can bring terrible struggles and wonderful strength that ensures we live this life to its maximum. It helps us to realise that one of the worst situation we can find ourselves in is facing death with regrets. That is why it is so important to love those who we value, to let them know their worth and importance in our life. To tell our loved ones how much they mean to us now, rather than wait until it is too late.

Another lady speaks of the death of her father and later, the sudden death of her brother. She was engaged to be married and the excitement of her father walking her down the aisle was ever present in her plans. A specific date had been thought of and was being discussed. However, she had a strong feeling that her father would not live long enough to fulfil that important role on that specific date.

MIRIAM'S STORY

"My father died on 29 July 1997. Although he died following a stroke there had been other complications. My fiancé and I had been exploring dates for our wedding. I wanted to choose the same date as my parents when they married. I felt the date, which would be in the year shortly after we became engaged, would be too soon. However, I had a strong conviction my father would not be able to walk me down the aisle if we waited another year. He was in poor health. I don't know why the conviction was so strong, but I really felt it and spoke my concerns. My fiancé agreed and we married on 21st August. My father took ill in October and eventually died on 29 July the following year. Being brought up as a Catholic I really struggled with his death and believed he was not in Heaven. It took me three years to begin to accept his death. I was angry with the belief system I had been brought up with.

I later chose to adopt the religion of Spiritualism and was much comforted and helped by the belief in the afterlife. When my brother died suddenly of a massive brain haemorrhage, I still struggled with his death even though I knew it was only his physical body that had died. I recalled an earlier conversation I had had with my brother. Ten days before he died, an Uncle had died suddenly. My brother had told me that the way our Uncle had died was the best, as he himself would not like to be on a life support machine and if he ever was, he wanted the machine turned off. Although I knew his soul lived on I really struggled to cope with his death. I could feel him around me as there was a definite presence and I could smell his aftershave and the distinctive aroma of the cigarillos he smoked. Because of my struggle I had to request he stood back. For a year and a half I attended counselling to help me cope with his passing. My brother was only 49 years old when he died."

Miriam Fitzgerald, Dublin

As can be seen with Miriam's story her grief at her father's death was compounded by her belief system, which in fact added to the stress of his passing. Yet despite her belief in the afterlife she still struggled to cope with her brother's death. The act of seeking help in counselling had been such a benefit to her.

It is essential that we realise our life is of a human nature and as such we will suffer the gamut of emotions that can overwhelm us during these times. It may not be the death of a person but of a much loved animal. The emotions will be similar and just as traumatic.

PART III

OVERCOMING GRIEF

The symptoms of grief can be all-consuming, Recovery can be a long process. In this part, there is information on the types of grief and the various methods which may be helpful in dealing with grief's effects.

There is GRIEF which is the term applied to a loss; the internalisation of feelings and thoughts.

MOURNING which is the process of your thoughts and actions in adapting to the loss; the externalisation and visual display of grief.

BEREAVEMENT which defines the loss.

All are intertwined as the passage of time continues. They are companions and bedfellows along the path to recovery and eventually constitute the overcoming of the stages of grief. There comes a time of completion allowing a significant return to a life that is of a reasonable normality. In turn, there is the acceptance of the loss and the gradual progress that brings feelings of joy and hope for the future.

Some forms of grief are less spoken of such as DELAYED and ANTICIPATORY grief.

DELAYED grief can be summarised in the death being caused by extreme conditions, such as when the body is missing or so badly damaged or decomposed as to result in identification being impossible. This causes many people to feel that the death has not occurred and leads to a delay in the grieving process.

ANTICIPATORY grief is experienced when a person is aware that their loved one is facing death, especially when the illness is deemedterminal. This also affects the dying person as they too experience stages of grief as they battle their illness. It has been established by various research bodies that these types of grief can add to the positive and negative tendencies of the stages people go through when trying to come to terms of a loss. The positive in the case of Anticipatory is when the person has gone through grief while the dying person is still alive. It has helped the relative, who is often also the carer, to come to a greater understanding of their emotions and how to deal with them. Research has found that the person returns to normality in a shorter period of time. The deceased, too, has been able to express their emotions and wishes to their family and friends, which has a profound effect in their acceptance of their impending transition through death. It relieves them of the concerns that they will not cope after their passing.

Questions often pondered are;

"How long does grief last?"

. . .

No-one can really say as there are so many factors associated with the stages of grief. A person's strength or lack of strength of character and their emotional stability are contributory conditions which may help or hinder the process of recovery. I am sure many people will agree that there is no set time limit for grieving.

"How long should a person mourn?"

Again there is no concrete answer. It is said that mourning is easing when a person can think of the deceased without feeling pain. The sadness may still be present but it is changed in intensity. It seems to lack the depth to overwhelm as it did when in the early stages of grief.

Mourning is a process that requires overcoming certain components of grief. I use the acronym AWAR to describe them:

A stands for Accepting the reality of the loss
　W stands for Working through the grief
　A stands for Adjusting to the home or place where the deceased is no longer physically present
　R stands for Re-locating the emotions surrounding the loss and the first step to moving on in life.

"How can I go on living without them?"

. . .

The answer to this question cannot be made to fit everyone. The relationship to the deceased can have a great influence on the person who is to carry on living. This invariably has a bearing on how one will react. In the early stages of a loss this may be a question spoken repeatedly. Emotions are heightened and a way forward is unclear. The support of family and friends is of paramount importance. Should this question become the sole thought for an extended time, a need for professional help is warranted.

The statement, "I will never love another", is common. Yet as the wounds of pain etched in hearts begin to heal, the feelings of love slowly return. A new loving relationship may never be forth-coming but love can be found in new friendships. In respect of a pet, love returns unexpectedly as pets bring so much to enhance our lives. Seeing other pets remind us of the love shared and may lead a person to find a new pet, who may just be grieving for the loss of their human companion.

Running through the stories in this book I see the pattern where a death has prompted loved ones to seek more information and research the subject of eternal life, and to investigate the belief that life continues after death. Many find themselves visiting Spiritual centres and churches. Some even attend Mediumship awareness or development courses in a bid to understand what happens after physical death. Lives are changed forever when a death occurs and it changes again when the realisation that death is not final and that Love, which existed before death still exists after death, is suddenly a reality. Mediums feel that this great adventure in our physical world is the classroom where we learn so many lessons, cruel and joyful, before we graduate to the higher grade. Once there, all the reasons for our different lessons will become apparent and we will not only understand but know why they were important to our progress as we begin our eternal life in our true home, within the realms of Spirit.

. . .

It takes a huge effort and courage to admit that grief is threatening to overwhelm us. Taking the steps to seek help is the beginning of a new way of life. There are some good pathways to healing from grief. The services of a psychologist or grief counsellor can be of tremendous benefit to a persons' recovery. The closeness of a friendship can help to ease the pain of grief. Family are so important at such times but grief can either destroy or bring a family closer. Finding a way to tell someone how you feel can be the key to acceptance and recovery.

When a pet is involved, telling the right person is critical as many will feel that losing a pet is not like losing a person who was close and loved. Yet the pet may have been the only companion that a person had. Owning and loving a pet whether from childhood or in adulthood brings tremendous joy. It can even be a person's reason for living. It is unkind to think that the loss of a pet is any less hurtful than losing a loved one. At times it may be necessary to have the animal put to sleep to prevent suffering. This brings another burden, as the owner is left questioning whether it was the right time or whether they should have waited and tried other veterinarian solutions. Guilt consumes the mind to distraction and creates a barrier to the thinking process where good memories are stifled by the last moments or decisions.

Death is not final, I say again death is not final. As a medium I know that the consciousness lives on when the physical body is discarded. That means any physical symptom that the body felt is also discarded. However, the mind may retain some of the memories and feelings for a short time until it is realised that death has not succeeded in destroying the consciousness of the soul that has made its transition from physical to spiritual. This is the truth that everyone will find out eventually. No matter what colour, creed, religion or gender, all will return to the etheric realms and become instantly aware that the physical life was only the pathway to learning lessons that provided physical life experiences. How we behave in this physical world will determine our existence in the etheric. I am sure, like me, you will question this, especially when thoughts of people who behave in a despicable way in our world are permitted to be within a realm of love and peace. Yes, they do come to the same place as you or I but they will not be on the same level. The etheric world is vast and has many levels, just as it states in the Bible (In my Father's house there are many mansions). The lower levels are sometimes considered the darkness. In order for the so called 'wicked' to progress they will be encouraged to atone and accept that their behaviour was wrong and against the Creator's (God if you will) design for earthly life which should be steeped in the ability to love and be loved. They do have choices to make and will work with their own consciousness to grow and evolve into better souls or to remain in denial and darkness. The existence within the etheric realms is one of choice. Will you make the right choice? Start now and be the best you can be while living in this physical world. Kindness, compassion and showing love are not signs of weakness but of strength within that can overcome obstacles and fears. How much more will your life be enhanced when you know that your words or actions have brought joy or support to another person or animal. What we make of this life is well within our own hands and capabilities. How we choose to live or die is ours to dictate. Illnesses that seek to disrupt our path can only do so if we allow them to. That is why we see some people survive while other succumb. I know this may be contentious but if we think carefully, many situations and things that happen in our life are of our own doing. Many prefer to blame someone or something rather than taking personal responsibility for what occurs in their life. Hard as it may seem it is essential to our development to understand our own faults as well as our good points.

Grief has a habit of ensuring every little thought, good or bad, comes to the surface when we find ourselves trying to comprehend the meaning of a death or even the cause. This, along with the other thoughts such as guilt, shame or fear tend to multiply the anguish and hurt we are battling hard to deal with.

Denial can be torture or pleasure. It is easy to deny the death ever happened and keep it from our mind but truth will never accept denial in any form. Sooner or later the death will intrude in such a way that acceptance is inevitable. The pleasure of denial is short-lived. The torture continues until there comes a moment in life when we are forced to continue living and free ourselves from the downward spiral of grief. We create a compass or a plan to shake us from the shackles of pain and allow the treasured memories to break though and suppress the tears in order that we may think of our loved one again in a more agreeable and joyful way. What we come to realise is that grief is the price we pay for loving someone or some animal that was a treasured pet and companion. The deeper the love, the greater the grief.

Spirit message:

"My child, as you feel the love within your heart, do remember it does not settle only in the heart but traverses the full body, penetrating into each cell and spreading outward in a way that can be seen by those who surround you. Be ever mindful when you share love that it too

will permeate into the body of the receiver. What a beautiful way to help others heal. To share love in an unselfish act or in speaking kind words. How your world would see a real change, lifting the clouds of despair and darkness and creating a flow of pure light and love.

Be that light in the dark, for many are in need and seeking it."

Blessings to you
   Chang-Li

In trying to find a way out of grief, the path taken can be laden with pitfalls. A good day can easily turn into a bad one with a sudden realisation that your loved one is no longer present in your life. This can be a simple thought of them in your head, such as when you are doing housework and you remember how they would help or maybe distract you. A bad day can just as easily turn good when you find yourself searching for something and discover an old photograph that brings a happy memory and makes you smile or laugh.

When grief is threatening to tear you down with the hurt, sadness and loneliness, give yourself a break. Be kind to yourself and know that your loved one will be feeling your emotions and longing to see you happy and well, enjoying life again. In fact, the perfect tribute to your loved one is to go on living, for them as well as yourself. To love deeply once again is a testament to the love you had for them. Yes, you may feel you are betraying their memory but let me tell you, your loved ones, including pets, are living safely and are well, within the etheric realms. Their wish for you is that you find peace and happiness as you continue living through your life. You will meet again and what joy there will be as the welcome party wait with open arms to guide you home.

. . .

I should explain at this point that if you were married to more than one husband and love was a constant, then they will all be there to greet you. There are no jealousies in the spirit world. If you were with an abusive partner you can rest easy, they will not be there to meet you as it is love that brings you together not abuse, violence or control.

Balancing the good with the bad days can be a chore but once there is acceptance and the realisation that what is happening is the direct result of grief, then comes the gift of learning to overcome it.

Our emotions tend to complicate things or cause us to over-think the silliest of small matters. Grief heightens this procedure.

PROCESSES OF GRIEF

INITIAL FEELINGS
Shock, Panic, Numbness Fear, Denial, Anger

RE-ACTIONS
Emotional outbursts, Dis-organised Searching for answers, Depression, Guilt, Loneliness

SETTLING
Acceptance, Affirmation, Hope

ADJUSTMENT
New patterns, New strengths, New relationships, Helping others

This process is not set in stone but most are present as we live through grief. The importance of family, friends or a confidante are critical to anyone who is experiencing a loss of any kind. To have that opportunity to express the pent-up emotions that threaten to tip the most sensible person over the edge is vital to the coping mechanism that can help us recover.

There are so many types of loss and grief is not just solely the domain of death. We can find ourselves grieving for the loss of a child or children, not through death but when they are old enough to leave home. I have listed some forms of loss:
The loss of the opportunity to raise children
The loss of a marriage through divorce or separation
The death of a pet
The loss of innocence
The loss of security
The loss of face
The loss of bodily functions
The loss of a limb(s)
The loss of faith
The loss of hearing/eyesight
The loss of hair/appearance
Aging
Still Birth
Abortion
Cot death
Unemployment
Retirement
Loss of income
Loss of credit
Miscarriage

These are some of the different sorts of loss and how they can lead to grief. Of course, there are situations and factors that can add to grief making it more difficult. Those listed below are no guarantee that problems will exaggerate the grief felt but their presence might alert us to possible difficulties.

1. The nature of the death:

Uncertainty over whether the death has occurred.
Unnatural, violent, messy death
Sudden death
Untimely death
Unrecognised death
Unmentionable death
Preventable death
Multiple deaths
Death accompanied by many other losses.

1. The nature of the relationship with the deceased:

An extremely close relationship
An ambivalent relationship
Great dependence

1. The nature and circumstances of the bereaved person:

Their psychological strength
How they have coped with previous losses
The presence of other stresses
Social support
Presence of a confidant(s)
Sex-conditioned beliefs
Idiosyncratic needs
Cultural background
Health
So many situations and conditions come together to add

more burdens to the already hard realities that grief brings. It is no wonder that those left to grieve find themselves falling into a darkness that seems to stifle any light that may try to penetrate the moments. A happy memory is destroyed by the constant images of the death that resurface in the mind.

Bringing light back into a life that is slowly disintegrating is not easy. A strong family bond or a close friendship is vitally important for support and for encouragement. Loneliness is a step that takes us deeper into the darkness and that is why human touch and contact has the ability to lift someone out of the shadows of grief and into the light of day. A smile can bring comfort and a simple "hello" or "how you doing?" can open an avenue to conversation.

Expressing your feelings by talking helps to lessen the load. The statement "A burden shared is a burden halved" is so true. Yet, as time passes, we often hear the words "It's been a while now, are you not over it?" I feel this is a cruel thing to say although I am sure when said it is not meant to hurt. I have said before no-one gets over grief, we just learn to cope and live with it.

There are some things that are not helpful when coping with grief. Here are a few:

Try not to get caught up on sorting everything at once. Take small steps, like creating targets that are achievable.

Try not to focus on changing things that just can't be changed. Focus on making yourself feel better.

Try not to sink into loneliness or feel that there is no-one to help; there are organisations and support groups available.

Try not to use alcohol, gambling or drugs to drown out your sorrow as these will only lead to poor mental and physical health.

Try to not to push yourself into working long hours in order to help forget your grief. This will only help for a short time and all it does is prolong your acceptance and delay any chance of recovering. Find a balance that allows time to care for your own needs.

Try not to allow thoughts of your loved ones' last days or moments to be the prominent memories. Recall the happy and fun times, the special occasions that brought joy.

As a medium, I think it is good to remind those who are missing a loved one that the deceased too are missing them. I know my beliefs may not be acceptable to everyone, but the knowledge that life is eternal and one day I will be with them again is such a massive comfort to me. My hope is that more people will come to understand and accept that death is not the end.

We live in an ever-changing world that is forever progressing, sometimes towards a better future and sometimes with a feeling of going backwards. Yet we all find ourselves moving on, many at a fast pace, while others are slow to catch on. Interacting with others is a necessary component to ensure life is not miserable or difficult. The human touch is a wonderful healer for all situations and conditions. I have already stated that in our childhood, when we hurt, we ran to our loved one and the cure was often "Let me kiss it better". That connection is so needed at times of loss. A kiss may not heal grief immediately but it will encourage a person to have hope and know that they are loved.

Our physical lives are affected by births and deaths. In the realms of Spirit these occasions are felt just as deeply. I would urge those who are grieving to be aware that life is eternal and as the physical world continues, so too does the etheric world. It is all around us. I read the following once in a small book:

"It is a glorious thing to move without fatigue from sphere to sphere. Spirit is so wonderful, and cannot be measured by space or confined within walls. The glorious truths of eternity are not easy to explain, but they burst upon you in a flash when the veil is lifted".

And

"It seems too terrible that those on Earth should mourn for the loved one departed, yet really so near".
(These words are from the book, *My Letters From Heaven* by Winifred Graham).

How true these words are, as they confirm that the etheric world is all around us and not in some far-away place or up in the sky.
Our human-ness makes us individual, but our Soul makes us unique. Science may find ways to clone animals and even humans, but they will never create a Soul. That is God's work.

PART IV

HEALING THROUGH MEDIUMSHIP

Working in service to Spirit has been an incredible journey for me. I have travelled to many towns and cities in the UK, visited and served in Spiritual Churches and Centres in the USA, Australia, Germany, Netherlands and Ireland. However, I feel it has been the messages that brought comfort and healing to people that have affected me in ways hard to describe. The change in people's faces and demeanour after receiving a message from their loved one in Spirit makes my service as a Spirit Medium all the more important. I find it essential in helping someone to come to terms with their loss and to begin to live again, knowing they will one day be re-united. The path to healing our grief and damaged emotions is littered with challenges. The simple message from a loved in Spirit to say, "I am safe and alright" allows the one who grieves to take the first step on the road to acceptance and recovery.

As I look back on my journey, I remember some of the messages that were so profound yet so comforting to those who were grieving. One in particular tells of a mother who found a way to cope with her son's death and her grief by not only joining various groups, but by training and developing her own group in order to help others in similar situations.

Rev. Kathleen's Story

Kathleen was left to bring up her children on her own as her husband fought his battle with drug addiction. Her son, Benjamin, was a very smiley, happy young boy but around four years old, he began to show symptoms of ADHD (attention deficit hyperactivity disorder). Benjamin was prescribed medication which was supposed to help. Sadly, as he grew, his condition deteriorated. As he attended senior school he seemed to be doing better. He was taken off the medication and didn't want to go back on it.

In eighth grade, after doing well, he started to get into trouble and was tested for drug abuse. Benjamin's drug abuse caused him to act strangely. His personality changed and he struggled with bouts of depression. When he began to use hard drugs, Kathleen had to make the difficult decision to have him leave the house. She found it hard to keep in touch as he would sofa hop from one friend's house to another. Kathleen did everything she could, trying various groups in search of help. The international group Al-Anon was instrumental in helping Kathleen accept that she had to learn to let Benjamin go - a heart-breaking decision. She also learned to focus on her own life and to accept the things she could not change and change the things she could. She found the wisdom to know the difference through the interaction with this group.

Benjamin passed away as a result of drug abuse in 2015. It was then Kathleen found the group called BALM (Be A Loving Mirror), who provided a recovery programme for people to help them deal with family members with an addiction. She trained in their methods and while finding her way through her grief, she developed her own programme/support group with BALM. Her dedication to this group and her compassion for people who were suffering through similar situations has been a pathway to her own healing from the grief of losing her son. It helped her to take back control of her life. She learned to set boundaries, to love in a detached way and to understand dis-ease in one's self. Kathleen's belief in life hereafter was present while she was pregnant with Benjamin. She joined the First Spiritualist Church of Onset, Massachusetts, where she continues to serve in her capacity as a Spiritual Minister.

The group Al-Anon is a satellite branch of Alcoholics Anonymous who are dedicated to assisting family and friends of addicts to understand, to cope, and to deal with the fallout from those who are embroiled in addictive behaviour.

Kathleen's story reminds me how important it is to acknowledge our own emotions and weaknesses and to find the courage to reach out when grief becomes unbearable or overwhelming.

On another occasion I recall visiting a small community hall, where I met a lady who was grieving the loss of a Grand-daughter. I had been called to time by the chairman, but I knew I had one more message from a very young and excited child. Her energy made me feel like skipping around the hall. She filled me full of bounce and fun. I knew this little Spirit girl was desperate to let her Mummy know she was "all better". I gave out the information that this little girl had only died a few weeks earlier and that she had been afflicted with various conditions that made her life less than perfect. Once her Grandmother raised her hand to acknowledge the little girl and the information, her Grand-daughter proceeded to give me the name, Mary (not her real name). This was the Grandmother's name. She went on to explain how she died and how she could now skip and she could swim. She spoke of her father's sadness and struggle to cope with her death. All this was confirmed by Mary. The most convincing message she gave was that she wanted her mother to know that she could "see" her. The whole audience gasped as Mary explained that her little Grand-daughter had been born blind and one of her greatest wishes was to be able to swim. Almost everyone had tears in their eyes. I suddenly realised that, as I spoke this little girl's words, the hall was totally silent. The effect of this message was written across Mary's' face. She spoke to me after the service to say how grateful she was to know her little Grand-daughter was well and happy. She now felt able to accept her death. She would be so happy to pass on the message to her daughter-in-law, the little girl's mother.

A message like this makes any medium's job so worthwhile. The hope that is within such emotional messages is a constant reminder of how grief can be eased with a few simple words from a loved one in Spirit.

On my pathway I found that some men were often dragged along to a Spiritual Church or centre by their partner or a friend and really were not interested nor had a belief in life after physical death.

Here I relay one particular instance. This message was extremely important to a young man, a soldier who had lost several fellow soldiers in Afghanistan. He had been dragged along to the Spirit church by his girlfriend. During the service he was laughing and two ladies complained. Suddenly I could hear myself say, "It's alright ladies, I am coming to him next". The colour drained from his face when I gave the name of one of his deceased soldier friends. I went on to pass the words of his friend and I could see him becoming emotional. The soldier speaking from the Spirit world told him all about the ambush and how his soldier friends had no chance of survival. He chastised the young man, telling him there was nothing he could have done to prevent his and the others' deaths. In fact, if he had been with him he too would be speaking through myself. He did make the young man smile when he told him how he had watched him and some soldier friends meet up in a pub and lift a glass to the memory of those who died. He laughed when he said an empty chair was in place for him and he had sat there, but they didn't know and couldn't see him.

As soon as the service finished, the young man ran out of the room and went into the gents' toilet. I went and spoke to his girlfriend to ask if he was alright. When he came out of the toilet, I said I had one more thing to say to him from his friend in Spirit. It was very personal and I wouldn't recite it here but the soldier went pure white in the face and said "Yes", then ran out of the hall. I knew without a shadow of doubt that this young man had now been made aware of the existence of the afterlife and that his fellow soldiers were in fact, still keeping loyal to their soldier friends who were still serving in their respective regiments.

A postscript to this message happened on my way home as the Spirit soldier remained with me, asking me to tell his friend more information. When I got home, I wrote down all the Spirit soldier had said in a letter and placed it in a sealed envelope. I had no idea if I would ever meet the young man again. Two years later I was back serving that Spirit church and I told the chairwoman about the soldier and the letter. To my amazement she told me she knew the young man and his mother was in the audience. I was able to pass the letter to the mother, who told me her son had lost another soldier friend and was struggling to cope. I knew the contents of the letter would bring comfort to the soldier.

On another occasion I was contacted by a young woman who asked me for a reading. I called at the woman's home where I found two women waiting. The woman who booked the reading, I will call Sheila (not her real name). The other woman was her mother who I will call Mary (not her real name). As soon as I began, I sensed the presence of a woman (I will call her Ann - not her real name) and I knew she was Sheila's sister. I explained that Ann was telling me about a bad car accident. Ann had died, but not at the scene or time of the accident. She was horribly injured but had survived for a time until her injuries eventually caused her death. Ann was showing me an empty wheelchair. Sheila and Mary became emotional and confirmed the accident left Ann in a wheelchair. Sheila and Mary were in tears. As Ann continued to tell me about herself and how she was free of pain and walking again, Sheila and Mary began to smile. Ann's carefree nature was so evident and her sense of fun shone through as she recalled happier times. Soon Sheila and Mary were laughing. Both were so grateful to know Ann was living on in Spirit as well as in their hearts. Once again, I was privileged to pass on Spirit's message of comfort, hope and love to both Sheila and Mary and allow them to pick up the broken pieces of their hearts and begin to live again, even though grief was still clearly visible in their mannerisms. The knowledge that Ann was no longer in a wheelchair was so important to them as they explained to me Ann was a very active and adventurous woman.

. . .

We must understand that a message from Spirit is very personal to the receiver and the communication can be of a very intimate nature. That is one reason why mediums often do not understand the message or what it means. Really it is not for the medium to understand or to try to put an interpretation on it. I have often gone wrong with a communication when I did this.

Spirit messages can come from animals too. I am not saying I am the Mrs Doolittle of the mediumship world, but I have brought comfort to some people by giving evidence of the survival of a much-loved pet or animal.

One occasion saw me visit a lady's home who was with a friend called Jane (not her real name). The lady, who was called Helen(not her real name) explained that she had suggested to her friend Jane that she speak with me. It was obvious by Jane's face that she was extremely sad and upset. Helen told me she had suffered a bereavement quite recently and wondered if I could help. I sat and spoke to Jane and very soon became aware of her mother drawing close form the Spirit world. I told Jane this and gave her information from her mother which Jane acknowledged. I could tell Jane was close to tears and offered to stop the conversation, but she wanted me to carry on. I became aware of a large dog which had a gentle nature and was sitting close to Jane, looking at her with such love in its eyes. I explained to Jane what I was seeing. I also told her I could see a bottle of a well-known alcoholic drink. I was puzzled by this, but Jane's face broke into a huge smile as she told me the name of the alcohol was the name she had called her dog. The dog had died recently and Jane was inconsolable. Although the presence of her mother was important, it was the presence of the dog that Jane had wanted. She explained she had had the dog since it was a small puppy. It was her constant companion in life. She was struggling to cope with the loss of the dog. I went on to let her know that I was aware she had to make the awful decision to have the dog put to sleep as it was so poorly. When she realised that the dog was close to her and still adored her, she began to relax her shoulders and smile again. I was able to speak to Jane to let her know pets and animals cross what mediums call "the rainbow bridge" into the Spirit world and that one day she will be with the dog again, but in the meantime she should recall all the happy times and know the dog is well and that her decision to let the dog go was the correct one to make.

Animals who have died find ways to let me know they are close to their humans in various ways. I remember a rabbit thumping its back paw loudly on the floor of the Spirit centre. I was in the middle of a demonstration and speaking to a woman when I kept hearing this thump, thump, thump. Then I became aware, in my mind, of the rabbit in front of the woman. I could see its back paws and noticed they were unusually large. I told the woman what I was seeing and she confirmed it was her pet rabbit and yes, he had huge back paws.

Another occasion had me laughing when I was made aware of a corn snake in Spirit. The images I was seeing confused me as alongside the corn snake was a packet of Kellogg's cornflakes. The owner of the snake made everyone laugh when she said the corn snake had been her pet and she had called it KELLOG.

Not all messages are willingly received and there was one occasion when I was given the image of a man in Spirit who impressed upon me a picture of him behind prison bars. I felt rather uncomfortable as this Spirit man drew close to me. It is not my place to judge and I knew he had something to say to a woman in the hall. It was not for me to pick and choose which message I would relay. My own experiences helped me understand that sometimes our loved ones or those we knew who had died were not, shall we say, as" kind" as they should have been when on this earth. Yet they still need to be heard. This man wanted to apologise to a woman for his behaviour towards her. He even told me it was unlikely she would accept his apology. He gave me no indication of what he had done but it was obvious he had been given a prison sentence for his actions. In fact, he had died in prison. I duly passed on his message to the woman and just as he had said, she didn't want to know. I had to explain that it was not my intention to cause her any pain or hurt but that sometimes those in Spirit need to work through their issues and try to progress by accepting they were wrong. This man's apology was his way of trying to make amends. The woman told me later what had occurred, and her biggest fear was that this man in Spirit would be able to have contact with her baby in Spirit. Thankfully I was able alleviate her fear as her mother in Spirit informed me she was caring for the baby.

A message like this is difficult for all concerned. It goes such a long way towards a better understanding of how a belief in life after physical death and the work of Spirit Mediums is so profound and so crucial to helping and encouraging those who are grieving to see a way forward. To walk through the darkness to light.

As a medium it is essential that I take into consideration the emotional state of any person who comes to me for a reading. Almost all of them are coming because they have suffered a bereavement and all they really want to know "Is their loved one alright?" To be able to work and be guided by those in Spirit, who are the ultimate carers, and bring such messages of comfort, healing and love to them is such a privilege.

I am so fortunate to be trusted by so many people in the physical and Spiritual worlds.

The messages I have included in this book are only a small percentage of the messages I have been called upon to give from those in Spirit. Knowing the importance of such words of comfort and giving the evidence that a loved one is existing in another word, safe and contented, is so crucial to helping those who are suffering through their grief.

The human body, with all its functioning organs and its mind, can become so distressed and ill when traversing through the stages of grief. The road to recovery and some sense of normality is long and hard, full of pitfalls and good intentions by others but still the path cannot be travelled by others. Those who grieve tend to feel so alone and feel that their pain will never ease. The darkness that descends upon them seems to grow heavier and heavier until the light of life is all but extinguished.

My service as a medium will not always be the answer, but when it is sought, I and my loving Spirit guides and friends will always do what is best to ensure loved ones are reunited for that short time. How fortunate am I to be permitted to play a small part in bringing Spirit messages of love and hope to those most in need, not to mention the bringing together of loved ones whom physical death has separated. I am ever so grateful for my gift and for the trust Spirit has in me.

I close this book with the words, "Death is a journey to Eternal life and no-one travels alone".

HELPFUL ORGANISATIONS

CRUSE Bereavement Counselling Service https://www.cruse.org.uk
Https://www.childbereavementuk.org
Https://www.mind.org.uk
Https://www.samaritans.org
Https://www.griefuk.org
Https://www.animalsamaritans.org.uk
Https://www.bluecross.org.uk

ABOUT THE AUTHOR

About the author:

Eleanor Walker lives in Perth, Scotland. She has been aware of Spirit since childhood. Fulfilling a childhood wish, she chose a career as a Police Officer before retiring after 27 years' service. She further developed her medium-ship with Spiritual mentor Agnes Pearson and went on to complete Medium Gordon Smith's Intuitive Studies Course. He, along with Spirit Medium Janet Parker, have been instrumental in her advancement in Mediumship Demonstrations. She serves Spirit Churches and Centres, Nationally and Internationally. She is a qualified Pet Bereavement Counsellor and holds a Diploma in Colour Therapy.

Printed in Great Britain
by Amazon